THE GREAT GATE

Rangjung Yeshe Books 🢒 WWW.RANGJUNG.COM

PADMASAMBHAVA 🢒 *Dakini Teachings* 🢒 *Advice from the Lotus-Born* 🢒 *Treasures from Juniper Ridge*

PADMASAMBHAVA AND JAMGÖN KONGTRÜ 🢒 *The Light of Wisdom, Vol. 1* 🢒 *The Light of Wisdom, Vol. 2*

YESHE TSOGYAL 🢒 *The Lotus-Born*

GAMPOPA 🢒 *The Precious Garland of the Sublime Path*

DAKPO TASHI NAMGYAL 🢒 *Clarifying the Natural State*

TSELE NATSOK RANGDRÖL 🢒 *The Heart of the Matter* 🢒 *Mirror of Mindfulness Empowerment* 🢒 *Lamp of Mahamudra*

CHOKGYUR LINGPA 🢒 *Ocean of Amrita* 🢒 *The Great Gate*

JAMGÖN MIPHAM RINPOCHE 🢒 *Gateway to Knowledge, Vol. 1* 🢒 *Gateway to Knowledge, Vol. 2* 🢒 *Gateway to Knowledge, Vol. 3*

TULKU URGYEN RINPOCHE 🢒 *Blazing Splendor* 🢒 *Rainbow Painting* 🢒 *As It Is, Vol. 1* 🢒 *As It Is, Vol. 2* 🢒 *Vajra Speech* 🢒 *Repeating the Words of the Buddha*

TRULSHIK ADEU RINPOCHE & TULKU URGYEN RINPOCHE 🢒 *Skillful Grace*

KHENCHEN THRANGU RINPOCHE 🢒 *Crystal Clear* 🢒 *Songs of Naropa* 🢒 *King of Samadhi* 🢒 *Buddha Nature*

CHÖKYI NYIMA RINPOCHE 🢒 *Present Fresh Wakefulness* 🢒 *Indisputable Truth* 🢒 *Union of Mahamudra & Dzogchen* 🢒 *Bardo Guidebook* 🢒 *Song of Karmapa*

TSIKEY CHOKLING RINPOCHE 🢒 *Lotus Ocean*

TULKU THONDUP 🢒 *Enlightened Living*

ORGYEN TOBGYAL RINPOCHE 🢒 *Life & Teachings of Chokgyur Lingpa*

TSOKNYI RINPOCHE 🢒 *Fearless Simplicity* 🢒 *Carefree Dignity*

DZOGCHEN TRILOGY COMPILED BY MARCIA BINDER SCHMIDT *Dzogchen Primer* 🢒 *Dzogchen Essentials* 🢒 *Quintessential Dzogchen*

ERIK PEMA KUNSANG 🢒 *Wellsprings of the Great Perfection* 🢒 *A Tibetan Buddhist Companion* 🢒 *The Rangjung Yeshe Tibetan-English Dictionary of Buddhist Culture*

THE GREAT GATE

A GUIDEBOOK TO THE GURU'S HEART PRACTICE

Chokling Dewey Dorje
Kyabje Dudjom Rinpoche
Tulku Urgyen Rinpoche
Chökyi Nyima Rinpoche

TRANSLATED BY ERIK PEMA KUNSANG

RANGJUNG YESHE PUBLICATIONS
KATHMANDU, NEPAL

Rangjung Yeshe Publications
Flat 2b Greenview Garden,
127 Robinson Road, Hong Kong
P.O. Box 1200, Kathmandu, Nepal

www.rangjung.com
office@rangjung.com
Copyright © 2008 Rangjung Yeshe Publications

1 3 5 7 9 8 6 4 2

First Edition 1987, second edition, 1989
Printed in the United States of America

Distributed to the book trade by:
North Atlantic Books & Random House, Inc.

Publication data: isbn-10: 962-7341-04-8 (pbk.)
isbn-13: 978-962-7341-04-8 (pbk.)

Authors: Chokling Dewey Dorje, Dudjom Rinpoche,
Tulku Urgyen Rinpoche.
Title: The Great Gate: A Guidebook to the Guru's heart
Practice: Translated from the Tibetan by Erik Pema
Kunsang (Erik Hein Schmidt).
1. Vajrayana liturgy (Rite)—Buddhism. 2. Buddhism—
China—Tibet. I. Title.

Cover Photo Graham Sunstein

TABLE OF CONTENTS

Preface

The four texts presented in this book are pertinent to every Vajrayana practitioner. Especially, they form a selection of liturgies and explanations connected with a cycle of teachings revealed in the last century by the great *tertön* Chokgyur Lingpa (1829–70).[1] These teachings, which fill more than ten volumes of books, are known as *Barchey Künsel* (The Dispeller of All Obstacles). The texts in *The Great Gate* form a basis for the preliminary practices a practitioner can undertake when feeling especially devoted to Guru Rinpoche, the Lotus-Born Master.

The Barchey Künsel Teachings

The 1st Jamyang Khyentse Wangpo (1820–92) described the *Barchey Künsel* cycle of teachings as follows:

> This present teaching belongs to the short lineage of *terma*. A countless number of different terma traditions, both the Early and the Later, have appeared, but I will now describe the present one.
>
> Manjushri in person, King Trisong Deutsen, had three sons. The middle prince was Murub Tseypo Yeshe Rölpa Tsal, a master on the tenth *bhumi*.[2] His reincarnation, authenticated by the triple means of valid knowledge and extolled by all sublime beings, was the indisputably

great treasure revealer and king of the Dharma, Orgyen Chokgyur Dechen Lingpa, who discovered an ocean like number of profound termas. These termas were linked with the tantric scriptures, established by the logic of fact, adorned with the experience of oral instructions, and endowed with the warmth of wondrous blessings.

Chokgyur Lingpa revealed this terma of *Barchey Künsel* from beneath the *vajra* feet of the Great Glorious One[3] at Danyin Khala Rong-go, the sacred place of the qualities of enlightened body. This was on the tenth day of the waxing moon of the ninth month in the Year of the Male Earth Monkey, when he was twenty years of age.

Keeping it secret for eight years, he applied it in his own practice. Later on, in connection with a perfect coincidence of time and place, he was accepted by the wisdom body of the glorious Dharma king of Uddiyana and consort, who bestowed upon him the empowerments and oral instructions, as well as special predictions and confirmations. From that time forward, Chokgyur Lingpa gradually let the terma of *Lamey Tukdrub Barchey Künsel* flourish.

This terma cycle is the essence of the heart of Padmakara, the knower of the three times, and is the most unique treasure concealed under the earth in Tibet. It is like the great treasury of the universal monarch, completely and unmistakenly filled with all the means for accomplishing the supreme and common *siddhis*.

In terms of the sections of tantra, this profound path is based on the great king of tantras, the *Peaceful and Wrathful*

Manifestations of the Magical Net of the Vidyadhara Gurus,[4] which is the root of blessings belonging to the category of the Eight Sections of the Magical Net.[5] Due to the certainty of oral instructions, there is no conflict in the fact that it also belongs to the category of Lotus Speech among the eight teachings of *sadhana* sections.[6]

In short, it is like the extracted essence of the meaning of all development and completion stages, as well as the activity applications of the tantra and sadhana sections.

In his book, *The Life and Teachings of Chokgyur Lingpa,* Orgyen Tobgyal Rinpoche narrates:

Chokgyur Lingpa showed Jamyang Khyentse the yellow parchment scroll of *Tukdrub Barchey Künsel, Sheldam Nyingjang* and his other terma teachings. Concerning these, Khyentse said, "I too have a terma teaching called *Tukdrub Deshek Düpa* with the same meaning as yours; even the words are identical. We should therefore make them into one. Mine is a mind treasure and yours an earth treasure, which is more auspicious." Thus, Jamyang Khyentse's terma was combined with Chokling's, and *Tukdrub Barchey Künsel* was a treasure common to them both.

Jamyang Khyentse then told Chokling to commit to writing all the termas not yet written down. Khyentse became the secretary, transcribing a great part of Chokling's terma teachings. This is why Jamyang Khyentse has written so many of Chokgyur Lingpa's termas.

They once performed a terma practice together and both had the vision of meeting Guru Rinpoche and Yeshe Tsogyal in person. Jamyang Khyentse and Chokgyur Lingpa had not the slightest doubt about each other. Khyentse Rinpoche received all the empowerments and reading transmissions of Chokling's terma teachings, and he considered Chokling no different from Guru Rinpoche. Both became renowned as tertöns beyond any dispute, like the sun and moon.

The entire cycle of the *Barchey Künsel* termas take up the first ten volumes of the *Collected Treasures of Chokgyur Lingpa* (*Chokling Tersar*). These volumes contain a treasury of teachings, sadhanas, and supplementary rituals that are sufficient for attaining complete enlightenment.

The first volume of *Chokling Tersar* contains the root tantra *Sheldam Nyingjang*. The first chapter of this tantra is the historical narration telling how Guru Rinpoche transmitted the *Barchey Künsel* teachings to his close disciples at Samye 1,100 years ago. The 2nd Chokling's commentary on the preliminaries (in this book) includes a translation of this chapter.

The next volume of *Chokling Tersar* contains sadhanas and teachings connected to *dharmakaya* Amitayus on life-extension, and *sambhogakaya* Lokeshvara on various means of benefiting beings. The third volume contains the three versions of the guru sadhana connected to *nirmanakaya* Padmakara, the fire-*puja* rituals of the four classes of *dakas* and *dakinis,* liberation through hearing and reading,[7] and commentaries by Jamyang Khyentse Wangpo, Jamgön Kongtrül (1813–99), and Chokgyur Lingpa.

The rest of the *Chokling Tersar* volumes cover the specific teachings connected to each of the twelve manifestations of Guru Rinpoche, as well as the sadhanas for the four divinities who dispel obstacles—Tara, Achala, Dorje Bechön, and Mewa Tsekpa.

Guru Rinpoche practiced twelve different *yidams.* Having accomplished them, he manifested in twelve different forms. Included among the oral instructions particular for each of these twelve manifestations are teachings on fulfilling the four activities, the general stages of development and completion, *chö,* the six doctrines, and Dzogchen.

The preliminary practices explained in *The Great Gate* were arranged by Jamyang Khyentse Wangpo in order to prepare the practitioner for entering the higher stages of Vajrayana practice. For beginners, Guru Rinpoche also kindly taught a sadhana that condenses the entire *Barchey Künsel* into one single short practice—"The Concise Manual for Daily Practice"—which combines the gurus of the three *kayas* and the twelve manifestations in one mandala.

LINEAGE

The *Barchey Künsel* teachings were propagated by Chokgyur Lingpa himself and the chief recipients of his termas: Jamyang Khyentse Wangpo; the 14th Karmapa, Tekchok Dorje (1798–1868); Situ Padma Nyinche (1774–1853); Situ Padma Kunsang; Jamgön Kongtrül; Jedrung Rinpoche; Dabzang Rinpoche; Pawo Rinpoche; Palyul Gyatrül; Chokgyur Lingpa's two sons, Wangchuk Dorje and Tsewang Norbu; Karmey Khenpo; Pema Chogyal of Menyag, as well as many others. Among the second generation of lineage holders were the root gurus of most of the present great masters of the Kagyu, Sakya, and Nyingma schools, including the 16th Karmapa, Dudjom Rinpoche, Tulku Samten Gyatso, and Dzongsar Khyentse Chokyi Lodro.

When the 1st Jamgön Kongtrül compiled the *Rinchen Terdzö*—his outstanding work known as the *Treasury of Precious Terma Teachings*—he included the major part of the *Barchey Künsel* termas. Since the preliminary practices in *The Great Gate* are included within the *Rinchen Terdzö,* every master who has received that transmission is therefore automatically a holder of its lineage. In recent years the entire teachings of the terma known as *Barchey Künsel* have been transmitted by Dilgo Khyentse Rinpoche and Tulku Urgyen Rinpoche to more than sixty living *tulkus* and lamas.

The empowerment for the chief guru sadhana of *Barchey Künsel*[8] was among the primary transmissions given by the 16th Karmapa, Dilgo Khyentse Rinpoche, and Tulku Urgyen Rinpoche on their first visits to the Western world and to Southeast Asia. Moreover, the 16th Karmapa practiced the concise form[9] of this sadhana daily throughout his life. It is also one of the first sadhanas that Tulku Urgyen Rinpoche would transmit to his students for their individual practice.

In *The Great Gate,* the preliminaries entitled *The Seed of Supreme Enlightenment* are emphasized. Initially written by Jamyang Khyentse Wangpo, they were later expanded by Tsewang Norbu (the son of Chokgyur Lingpa) and by Karmey Khenpo Rinchen Dargye. The commentary by Chokgyur Lingpa's reincarnation explains how to put these preliminaries into practice. Recently, Tulku Urgyen Rinpoche condensed them into an even shorter version.[10]

In addition, there is an explanation, composed by Dudjom Rinpoche, of the outer, inner, and secret meaning of the supplication to Guru Rinpoche known as "Düsum Sangye." The supplication itself is a terma and is included in the liturgy for the preliminaries under the guru yoga section. Also included in this book are commentaries given orally by Tulku Urgyen Rinpoche at Nagi Gompa, his hermitage in Nepal, and by Chökyi Nyima Rinpoche.

The earlier edition of this book contained an extensive glossary. You can find it online within the large "Rangjung Yeshe Glossary" at WWW.RANGJUNG.COM.

This book would not exist if it weren't for the kindness of my teachers, Dilgo Khyentse Rinpoche, Tulku Urgyen Rinpoche, Chökyi Nyima Rinpoche, Chokling Rinpoche, and Orgyen Tobgyal Rinpoche. From the beginning to the end, their suggestions, teachings, help in translating the difficult points, and encouragement has been the sustaining force in the publication of this book. I would also like to thank Marcia Schmidt, Graham Sunstein, Zack Beer, Joan Olson, and Joanne Larson for all of their efforts in bringing forth this new edition.

The Four Mind-Changings

Tulku Urgyen Rinpoche

When putting the Buddhist path into practice, all the *panditas* of India and the masters of Tibet agree that we must purify our obscurations and gather the accumulations. Due to the vastness of the Dharma teachings, one person is unable to practice all of them. For this reason, the essence of all the sutras and tantras was condensed into four things to think of, the four mind-changings, and four things to practice, the preliminaries of four times one hundred thousand.

The basis for engaging in Dharma practice is taking to heart the four mind-changings: the reflections on the precious human body, death and impermanence, cause and effect of karma, and the defects of samsara. All the vehicles mention the precious human body, endowed with the eight freedoms and ten riches. The eight unfree states, however, are rebirth among the hell beings, hungry ghosts, animals, barbarians, long-lived gods, or living in a time without buddhas or among humans having false views, or being unable to communicate. Born in any of these eight circumstances, we are fettered by our conditions and lack the freedom to practice.

In the three lower realms—the hells and the hungry ghost and animal realms—one has no chance to practice Dharma. As a barbarian, a long-lived god, a person with wrong views, or an idiot, there is neither the thought nor ability to practice; one is not a suitable vessel for Dharma practice. A vessel is a place to put things. With no container, where can you pour your tea? Likewise, when born in one of the eight unfree states, one lacks the karma or fortune to practice.

One cannot practice in the hells because of the suffering of heat and cold. The hungry ghosts are unable to practice because of the suffering of hunger and thirst. The animals are too dumb and stupid to know how to practice. Barbarians are like the primitives who live on the border between India and Tibet. They do have a human form but wear no clothing except for a small belt; for food, they kill wild animals, which they eat raw.

The long-lived gods, who remain for one or two *kalpas* in the Realm of the Thirty-three on the top of Mount Sumeru, have no interest whatsoever in Dharma practice; the thought never enters their minds. They distract themselves in godly luxuries for the whole of their long life. One day, however, their life span ends, and like rain falling from the sky, they plummet to the lower realms. They can even plunge to the hells without an intermediate state.

Holding wrong views is another unfree state. Examples of wrong view are mistakenly thinking, "There is no karma, no cause and effect. How can there be buddhafields? Who has seen them? Who has returned from the hells? How can anybody know such things? There are no past and future lives; there are none of these things." If such a person met the Buddha himself, he or she would have no interest whatsoever.

Right now, we do not live in a time without buddhas. This excellent kalpa is a time in which buddhas appear and teach, and where the teachings last for some time. One thousand perfect buddhas will appear during this time. So far, only four have come; many more will come in the future.

A kalpa, the full time-cycle of our known universe, is divided into four parts: creation, abiding, destruction and voidness. Each lasts an equal amount of time, a very long time. We are now in the abiding kalpa. During this time, there are eighteen middle kalpas. Sometimes the life span grows longer and longer, the fortune greater and greater; then again it lessens, the lifespan gets shorter and shorter, everything becomes worse. Right now we everything is worsening. There are eighteen middle kalpas with a long kalpa at each end, making twenty in all. These twenty kalpas together make one fourth of a *mahakalpa*.

For as long as the abiding mahakalpa lasts, the kalpa of destruction also lasts. When the seven suns destroy everything, it becomes hotter and hotter, drying up rivers and burning mountains. Everything ends in total voidness. This state of voidness lasts for as long as the creation. Only now, during the kalpa of abiding, can we hear Dharma teachings. There is not any Dharma during creation, destruction, or the void. In any of these three kalpas, one is in an unfree state. Now, we are not in any of the eight unfree states; we have the eight freedoms.

We also have, as well, the ten endowments, which are the ten favorable conditions, five from oneself and five from others. The five from others are the following: The Buddha appeared, he taught, the doctrine survived, there are teachers, and they have the kindness to teach. These five together are considered to be the merging of external favorable conditions.

Among the five favorable conditions from oneself, the first is to be born as a human; the second is to be born in a central country, a place where the Buddhist teaching is being spread; the third is to have the five senses intact; the fourth is to have a rightful livelihood enabling one to enter the teachings; and the fifth is to have confidence and to take refuge in the Buddha, Dharma, and Sangha, the Three Precious Ones. With these five, the five favorable conditions from oneself are complete.

Now we have the five favorable conditions from others and the five from oneself. Not being born in the eight unfree states and having the ten endowments is truly a supreme human life. It is like a wish-fulfilling gem. Through this body, this precious human life, we have the good fortune to practice.

Though we have obtained the precious human body, it is like holding an old piece of chinaware in our hand; the moment it hits a stone, it completely breaks. It will not stay intact. I often quote, "As life is composite, it has no permanence." Life is impermanent. As I mentioned earlier, the external universe will be completely destroyed by the heat of the seven suns. However, cosmic annihilation is not the only thing to consider. Everyone will die. Even supreme individuals are impermanent. Consider past buddhas and bodhisattvas, the universal monarch of the golden wheel who ruled four continents, the universal monarch of the silver wheel who ruled three continents, the universal monarch of the copper wheel who ruled two continents, and the universal monarch of the iron wheel who ruled the Jambu continent. Where are these powerful beings now? Many Indian kings of the past could fly, never needing to walk on the ground. They could enjoy the seven royal possessions: the precious wheel, the precious jewel, the precious queen, the precious elephant, the precious horse, the precious minister, and the precious general. Some could visit Indra, the king of the gods, and sit together on the same throne. Of these fabled kings, only their names remain. Powerful people are also impermanent.

Contemplate further how life is impermanent due to the many causes of death. There are 404 sicknesses and eighty thousand evil forces that are circumstances for death. When the moment of death comes, you can put yourself in an iron chamber guarded by one hundred thousand soldiers but that will not ward off death. There is no protection from the Lord of Death. Beauty, heroism, and wealth are not death's equals. A pretty face cannot seduce death; bravery cannot vanquish it, and all the gold in the world is not a sufficient bribe. Nothing can be done; death is unavoidable.

Impermanence has four ends. First, the end of birth is death. No one born from a father and mother has yet survived death. Milarepa said, "As soon as you have a body, you have death. The only difference between being alive and being dead is one breath." The terrifying corpse is loathsome; yet it is our own body we are speaking of. Right now we are breathing and alive. In the space of just a single breath, we become a corpse. That death follows birth is the most significant point of impermanence.

Next, regardless of the inconceivable wealth and possessions one may amass, the end of hoarding is dispersion. Years ago in Tibet, a great merchant named Norbu Sangpo had so many mules that if one lined them up, they would reach from Lhasa to China, like a rosary stretching all the way without a break. Apart from his name, nothing remains now, not a single one of his possessions. All have vanished.

The end of meeting is separation. People gathered together in a city or a country or in any community, like the nuns who stay with me at Nagi Gompa or the members of a family, the husband and wife and children, are all like customers in a marketplace who come and go. Their staying together has no permanence. Although we are together now, we have no power to stay together forever. We are like people mingling in a dream. The end of meeting is separation.

The end of building is destruction. The houses built in the past never last more than a few thousand years at the most. They fall apart. Even though a house can withstand time for one or two thousand years, it will end in ruins.

We should really think about these four ends of impermanence, because they are a reality. The years pass by and will never return. The month that passed can only recede further and further. Moreover, in each short moment, we become older, and as time passes our life grows shorter. The Lord of Death is like the mountain's shadow coming closer and closer. The Lord of Death does not linger for even an instant; he always comes closer while our life span diminishes, without the power to remain still for even a second. We might not notice, but one day the Lord of Death catches up in the last moment of our life, and in the snap of a finger, our time is up.

The external world is impermanent; yesterday and today are impermanent. Right now is also changing in the three times. The times are in constant movement; we are spending our lives every

moment. Life only runs out. Right now, acknowledge impermanence and death.

Impermanence pertains not only to death, but also to enemies,
friends, and all relationships, which lack any stability. Nothing
stays as we know it for even an instant; change is constant. As
time runs out, we get older, friends and enemies change, cities
change, the local people change, and at home our family ages.
Nothing in the world endures. All things change. Buddha nature
alone is permanent and stable. Nothing else lasts (*laughing*)! Only
self-existing wakefulness is permanent.

Through impermanence, weariness arises. For example, if
one's father and mother die, or if one of a married couple passes
away, what anguish the one left behind must bear! This is true
even among animals. For instance, when the baby of a cow dies,
doesn't the mother suffer? Weariness and suffering are the same.
With such weariness comes the feeling "Now my time is running
out; what else is there to do but practice Dharma? Nothing else is
of any use, nothing at all." With deep revulsion clearly in mind,
unenlightened existence becomes unbearable. That is the meaning of weariness. Through renunciation, one recognizes, "There is
nothing in samsara with any permanence."

The five sense objects deceive us. The eyes, fascinated by form,
are like a moth diving into a flame. Set a butter lamp for an offering and these winged insects, attached to what they see, fly straight
into the flame and die, don't they?

The ears, fascinated by sound, similarly bring suffering.
Previously, in Tibet, hunters used very melodious flutes. Going
to the forests, they would play very sweetly, and the deer would

listen to the sweet music, while a hunter would slowly sneak up and kill them. The ear clinging to sound is like a deer killed by a hunter using flute and arrow.

The nose clinging to a smell is like a bee getting caught in a flower. A bee likes honey and the flower's fragrance. It goes into the flower to drink, and in the evening the flower closes and the bee dies inside, captivated and captured through its sense of smell.

The tongue's clinging to taste is like a fish caught by bait on a hook. The hook is thrown in the water. The fish, attracted to the bait, is caught, fascinated by a delicious taste.

When the body clings to touch, it is like an elephant drowning in a mud pool. An elephant is very heavy, so when it goes down in a big pool, it may be unable to get up and it dies there. Like this, if one clings to the five sense objects, they become enemies. Therefore, regard them as pointless, futile.

Through intense renunciation, endeavor in accepting and rejecting what concerns cause and effect. Accepting means taking up the white and virtuous actions as much as possible, and rejecting means abandoning the black, negative actions. Endeavor in this. The "white and virtuous" refer to the ten virtuous actions: three of body, four of speech, and three of mind. Without practicing the virtuous actions, they automatically become the ten unvirtuous ones. We must renounce the ten unvirtuous actions, and, having given them up, the ten virtuous actions are inevitably produced. If you think there is no cause and effect, then you lack understanding of positive and negative actions. This must be understood. If the cause is virtuous, the effect is also virtuous; one goes to higher realms, to liberation and enlightenment. If the cause is unvirtuous, negative, tied to the five poisons, then one will wander about in the three realms of samsara. Cause and effect is infallible, like the shadow that follows one's body wherever it goes.

Karma follows oneself like a shadow follows a body. To purify or get rid of this shadow, only recognition of and stability in the buddha nature can really help. Nobody else can throw karma away. No single person, not even the strongest man in this southern Jambu continent, has been able to cast away cause and effect and be freed from karma. To create white karma is to practice the true teachings. To create black karma is to engage in negative actions. Their effect is infallible. You will have to experience the results of karma, your own actions. You must really understand this.

Only self-existing original wakefulness, buddha nature, can bring karma to an end. When stable in self-existing awareness, or *rigpa,* karma, cause, and effect are exhausted. Karma cannot run around with self-existing wakefulness, which is free from causes and does not does not arise because of conditions. If a white or black cloud appears, does it change the sky? In the same way, self-existing wakefulness, or rigpa, is untainted by karma and by cause and effect. Whatever undergoes cause and effect, such as earth, water, fire, and wind, can be exhausted. But space is without cause and effect. Can anybody paint the sky red or white? In all other cases, there is cause and effect.

If one sincerely practices the ten virtuous actions as cause, then the effect is happiness in the higher realms and ultimately liberation in buddhahood. This is the happiness resulting from a virtuous cause. There are two things: truly high position, which refers to the higher realms of humans, *asuras,* and *devas;* and the true goodness, which is the level of buddhas and bodhisattvas.

By committing the ten negative actions, one produces the suffering of the three realms of samsara. The cause of liberation is to endeavor in the ten virtuous actions and to turn away from the ten negative actions. In the three lower realms of the hells, hungry ghosts, and animals, there is no happiness whatsoever. In the higher realms, the joy does not last. One alternates between joy and sorrow.

The three kinds of suffering are suffering of change, the suffering upon suffering, and all-pervasive suffering. What is the changing suffering? Suppose there was an earthquake and the houses crumbled. You can imagine how it felt. Parents died; fire burned everything; one is left behind alone as in wartime. Such things happen in this world. Yesterday, everybody in the family was together and everything was fine, but today, because of some sudden circumstances, one has no food to eat and nothing to wear. One walks around holding a stick and begging for something to eat. Suffering upon suffering is that, in addition to this misery, one gets leprosy, a *naga* sickness, or an illness like cancer.

What exemplifies the all-pervasive suffering? This suffering is that one draws closer to death with each passing moment. The beings of the three worlds are not aware of this, but the sublime beings perceive it. All the arhats, bodhisattvas, and buddhas know it, but sentient beings are not at all aware of the all-pervading suffering of formation. An example for the difference between the awareness of sentient and sublime beings, is like the difference between the awareness of having a hair on the hand or a hair in the eye. Sentient beings are like the hair on the hand. If you put a single hair in the palm of your hand, you will not feel much. Sublime beings are like hair in the eye. Put a hair in the eye and there is immediate awareness of it and the wish to remove it.

In the past, in Tibet, there was one man from Langro Plains who was depressed his whole life. His face never showed any other expression than sadness. He didn't suffer, but because he was aware that life was running out, he was called "dark face from Langro Plains." We should also consider impermanence and suffering, and taking its meaning to heart, blend it with our mind, not just keep it as a mere theory. We should actually assimilate the meaning in our heart.

TEACHINGS ON THE PRELIMINARIES

Chökyi Nyima Rinpoche

THE COMMON PRELIMINARIES

When it comes to realizing our innate nature, the four mind-changings are conducive circumstances. These four general reflections are helpful to make us more sincerely interested in actually practicing the Dharma. In particular, they are the way to turn our mind toward the essential truth, to what really matters.

The four mind-changings are not complicated to understand; small children can learn the four mind-changings. What we need is to personally take them to heart. Unless a wild horse has been tamed, you cannot ride it. It would be dangerous and harmful for the rider. In the same way, unless we have really taken to heart these four mind-changings, it is very difficult to make genuine progress in Dharma practice. The person who has not really reflected on the four mind-changings is like someone trying to ride a wild horse.

When you want to garden, isn't it true that you first need to prepare the soil? You have to remove stones and pieces of wood and soften up the hard lumps of earth. After that the soil can be receptive and ready for the seeds you will plant and water. Otherwise, you can throw seeds on the ground, but without the right conditions, they won't sprout. Even if they do, they won't produce a good plant. The four mind-changings require us to think about something that is very real. They are a practical way of loosening up the hardness of our tight minds. The way to know when the four mind-changings have really taken effect is when our attachment to things as being concrete and permanent has diminished, and our selfishness, arrogance, and conceit have decreased.

It is very easy to reflect on these four mind-changings; you don't have to be a great philosopher and think deeply. They are simple and direct. All of us need to remind ourselves often of these simple truths. When we really take to heart and assimilate the truths of the four mind-changings, automatically we become genuine practitioners. We have already been moved to some extent, all of us; otherwise we would not have any interest in the Dharma. To turn one's mind to the Dharma, to direct oneself toward practice, to tame and soften oneself is not as easy as simply hearing teachings on the four mind-changings, because they are quite uncomplicated. We need to take them to heart and assimilate them within our stream of being.

Through these four ways of changing direction, we become softer. Our rigid attitude gets loosened up. This is vital in order to practice the Dharma. It is through this that we open up to understanding what kind of shortcomings we have, and we become interested in changing them, in actually practicing, and in training in the Dharma. It is easy enough to understand the details of these four mind-changings, but to take them to heart requires some pushing; it requires some effort. Therefore, we need to remind ourselves, again and again, to consider these four facts.

Most of you have probably heard the teachings connected to

the four mind-changings quite a few times. It is entirely possible that if now you have to hear them one more time, you will sit and be quite bored! Nevertheless, the point is not to merely comprehend. Comprehending is very simple; just by hearing these teachings, we can understand them.

The four mind-changings are about pointing out facts that are obvious. We can easily understand that the situation we are in is somewhat fortunate compared to that of other beings. The precious human body is rare and valuable. Secondly, everyone knows that all things perish, that nothing lasts forever. There is nothing profound about it. Impermanence is an obvious fact. Thirdly, we understand that there are consequences to what we do. If we smile at someone, they smile back. If we frown and say nasty words, we get a corresponding response. If we do evil, there is an unpleasant feedback. If we do good, there is a positive return. There is a law regarding our actions, our karma. Finally, the fourth of the four mind-changings—that there are negative sides to samsara—is not that difficult to comprehend either. We create karma, we get involved in disturbing emotions, and something happens that doesn't feel good. Samsaric situations are not permanently pleasant. Isn't that is how life is?

The Precious Human Body

The first of the four mind-changings is about the precious human body, which means having a human body endowed with all of the factors that are conducive to spiritual progress; they are known as the eight freedoms and ten endowments. If we are born among hell beings, hungry ghosts, animals, asuras, and devas, we don't have the perfect circumstance for practicing the Dharma. What we really need to understand is that our precious human life is very difficult to obtain. In terms of cause, it doesn't happen by chance, without a reason, without something that goes beforehand. In fact, to end up as a human being this time around required incredible merit created in former lives. It is not only that; merit is not enough. The merit needed to be combined with pure aspirations. One must have made very sincere wishes to use that merit for something worthwhile, and after that one was reborn as a human with a precious human body.

These sincere wishes are especially evident in someone who wants to use his or her life to realize what is true, what is ultimately real. For such an individual, it is not enough to merely live an ordinary life. He or she is interested in learning and experiencing what is most important. The first point is interest in the truth. The second point is to want to carry through with that interest with perseverance, pursuing where and how one can come to understand the truth. Finally, there is the wish to assimilate the understanding created through study and reflection and by means of meditation practice. In other words, we need to have these three, the interest, the perseverance, and the insight to realize the ultimate truth. In short, to be someone who is sincerely interested in, who has the perseverance to pursue and the insight to realize the basic truth, requires a tremendous amount of merit combined with pure aspirations. Thereby one is reborn in a precious human body, in a form that is rare and extremely valuable!

If you look around in this world, how many life forms do you see? Not just a myriad of insects, but in the oceans as well, there are so many different kinds of beings of untold various sizes. There is such a huge number; an almost incalculable number of beings. Consider how many billions of human beings are present in this world. Among this large number of humans, how many actually have the sincere interest, the perseverance, and the insight to realize the ultimate truth? By examining in this way, we can see how extremely rare and precious the occasion to meet the Dharma is.

If we think like that, it is easier to comprehend the idea behind the analogy of the blind turtle on the big ocean; otherwise it seems like a strange example. Imagine that a blind turtle lives on a planet that is covered by water. On the surface of the water there is a wooden ring floating around. The turtle comes up to the surface only once every one hundred years. The chance of the turtle putting its head through that wooden ring is the same as the chance of someone getting reborn in a precious human body. Whether we consider the precious human body in terms of causes, in terms of numbers, or in terms of analogy, it is an incredibly rare and precious situation. Among all types of living forms, the best support for practicing the sacred Dharma is that of the precious human body.

To reiterate, the situation of having a precious human body does not happen by chance; it has causes. These causes lie in our past lives, during which we did good actions and formed an interest in true knowledge and compassion. Either we heard about knowledge and compassion, or we learned about them, thought about them, and wanted to know more. That formed the inclination; together with the good karma, it brought this result. Even though we were born in lots of different countries all over the world, we had an interest that brought us together in the Dharma. The power of ripening of karma is very strong. Some of people who attend my seminar came from far away and took a lot of trouble to come, because of strong interest. But there are people living close by who don't have that interest and therefore don't come to listen; that is called karma. Because of possessing this tendency from past lives, the continuation of this affinity shows itself now.

In short, to have obtained a precious human body is both exceptional and valuable. It is a rare achievement, because it is caused by a vast goodness done in our past. If we look around, how many people actually do great acts of goodness? Not many do so; from this angle we can see that it is unusual.

Impermanence

The second mind-changing is reflection on impermanence. That means we should appreciate and rejoice in what we have, but clearly understand that it will not last very long. The precious human body is extremely difficult to obtain and very easy to lose. If it were as difficult to lose as to obtain, you would be somewhat safe. When something is very hard to achieve, yet extremely easy to lose, one needs to be careful. When we appreciate that we have obtained something that is incredibly hard to find, there is a good reason to congratulate ourselves: "I have done well!" When it happens, this is excellent; we should sincerely rejoice in our situation. There is no need to discourage ourselves when we have achieved something that is tremendously valuable.

Now is the time to pay attention. Shantideva said in *The Way of the Bodhisattva* that this human body is like a ship we can use to take us to the other shore. If we don't use it properly this time around, we won't necessarily obtain it again. If you really think about this, it is time to wake up. Do not be stupid and waste this opportunity. If we have a ship to reach the other side, it is better to use it now. We need to make use of this human body to reach liberation, to be free. If there were no suffering or death, it would be okay. But there is suffering and death.

Perhaps if, at the time of death, we could take with us whatever we want, it would somehow be acceptable. If we could bring along a few friends, a few possessions, we would have something to hold onto. Unfortunately, as a fact of our mortality, when we die, we die alone. We are unaccompanied by anyone. We may not want to leave our possessions and family behind; yet we cannot take even one thing. It is tough. This will happen to all of us. Our family, our siblings, other relatives, friends, lovers, children, our reputation, our wealth: all of that will be left behind without a single exception.

From the moment we took birth from our mother's womb until we die, we have kept company constantly with our body. This physical body has been our servant; perhaps we have been its slave. We have worried a lot about getting too hungry or getting too cold, or too hot. We have done so much for it. We fed it daily, cleaned it, and tidied it up in all different ways. Yet, when we stop breathing, our body becomes a useless corpse. People will try to get rid of it as soon as possible. Other people will regard it as a disgusting, frightful, filthy thing.

In general, all composite things are impermanent. They don't last, but especially the human body does not last. A blade of grass and a piece of paper are regarded as very fragile, aren't they? But if kept well, they can last longer than a human body. The Buddha said, "All composite things are impermanent. Just as among all footprints, the footprint of an elephant is the largest, among all concepts, the concept of impermanence is the most eminent." When we really understand that all composite things do not last, our attachment to permanence becomes much less. Moreover our clinging to the fleeting pleasures of this life is diminished. When we begin to understand the reality of how all the things of this life change from moment to moment, we become more interested in, and direct our mind toward, the sublime truth.

Understanding impermanence loosens up our rigid clinging to a solid reality; it is weakened and reduced. Composite things are like the flickering of a star, like foam on water, like a mirage, like a reflection, like an echo, like a dream.

When someone is born, it is unavoidable that his body will eventually die; he can't help it. Whatever is gathered together will be spent, used up. Whatever is built falls apart, crumbles. You cannot prevent a gathering from dispersing. Everything is like that; it is the nature of things. The whole universe was first formed, then remained, and finally will disintegrate In short, whatever is formed necessarily also vanishes.

A human life is formed through causes and circumstances. It changes from moment to moment until in the end one dies. Milarepa said, "If you cannot take the fact of impermanence personally, you will not be a good practitioner." There are many causes for death and very few causes to sustain life. Therefore, don't postpone training in what is really true and meaningful; practice immediately.

All of us can understand that everything composite is impermanent; we can understand it very clearly, if we put our minds to it. We can understand that there is really no point in being too attached to the things of this life. Everything is like soap bubbles, or foam on water: what is the point of being so attached to a bubble? It is going to burst at any moment anyway.

When we look at ourselves, we can count how many years of our lives have passed. Honestly speaking, a lot of us here are not that young any longer. Since you cannot count on having a long life, it would be much better to be a little bit realistic about how to spend the rest of your time. Don't go around being scared about this. Simply be realistic and practical about how to use your life in a meaningful way. The thought of impermanence spurs us on toward Dharma practice.

When you find something that is very valuable, but fragile, it is better to make use of it as soon as possible. Take full advantage of the precious human body by learning, reflection, and meditation practice. Death is certain, but how and when are not. If we could settle on the number of years we have to live, we could sit down and make a program, right? Unfortunately, death comes unannounced. While eating, people die; while talking, they die. While suffering from sickness, they die. While lying down and sleeping, people die. Some get so sad that they die. Some, being too depressed, end their lives. Some are so happy, too happy; then they die! Sometimes people die from taking beneficial medicine; sometimes from taking useless drugs. It is never sure. Because all of this is not sure, it is better not to make plans such as "Next year I will practice," or, "After a long while, I will have more time; then I will really practice." It is better to practice as soon as possible, right away.

The clinging to something as being real, lasting, and concrete is the exact opposite of the understanding of impermanence. Moreover, the attitude that everything is permanent, real, and truly existing is in exact contradiction to how things actually are. There is nothing that lasts. There is no real thing. All the formed things only seem to exist as long as we don't look closely. Things are only real for the deluded mind. It's like while being asleep and dreaming. For the dreamer, whatever is dreamt seems to exist, seems to be real, concrete, and permanent. In fact, it is merely a dream. The dreamer is lying there snoring, dreaming the whole thing. It isn't real. But if we have to settle whether it is real or not, we must say that for the dreamer, it is real while dreaming.

What happens when that person wakes up? One discovers that it was only a dream; there wasn't anything to it. You can understand at that point that there wasn't any reality to it. However, at the same time, some people still prefer to cling to their dreams as having real value. If it was a pleasant dream, one holds onto that pleasantness for maybe a few hours or a few days! If it was a really nasty, ugly dream, one can make oneself unhappy about it for a few days.

Even though we know that dreams are unreal, they can still affect our mood and change it to either happiness or sadness. That is the power of habit. By waking up from a dream, the whole dream spectacle falls apart. In the same way, it is possible to wake up from the big dream of the three realms of samsara. The whole drama of deluded experience falls apart. When awakening from the sleep of ignorance, the knowledge that perceives the nature as it is and all possibly existing things unfolds. That is called buddhahood.

Everyone who meets together will again part. Whoever takes birth will die. Whatever is built will crumble, no matter how solidly it is built. Whatever is collected will be dispersed. A person who truly takes to heart the fact of impermanence becomes the foremost practitioner, like the great master Milarepa. He left everything, all mundane concerns, behind and practiced alone in caves, in forests, with incredible perseverance. He practiced the path of means, the six doctrines of Naropa, as well as the path of liberation, Mahamudra itself, day and night. Even when sleeping, he would continue his training in the luminosity of deep sleep. He threw away all selfish aims such as fame, praise, reputation, and so forth. He did not hold onto any self-oriented concerns. Within that very lifetime, he attained supreme accomplishment. Many other great masters had earlier given up all worldly concerns and went to the mountains and caves and focused one-pointedly on practice. Some of them would even, in a few years or within that same lifetime, attain accomplishment. Not just a few; there have been many like that.

It is said that someone who really understands impermanence is like a coward who discovers a viper in his lap. He is not going to wait until it leaves by itself; he will immediately jump up. Another example is a vain girl who discovers her hair is on fire. She will act immediately, not waiting until some other sweet, good time.

Reflecting on impermanence helps us to understand emptiness, the emptiness of all things. Reflecting on impermanence helps us to understand that everything is futile to pursue. Being more detached and having less craving come automatically through understanding impermanence. Furthermore, understanding impermanence will diminish our selfish emotions. Understanding impermanence will pull us closer to realizing the ultimate attainment. In this way, there are an incredible number of benefits from reflecting on the fact that nothing lasts. Do not simply reflect on this; take it to heart as something real. Do not only endeavor to understand impermanence intellectually and talk about it; really take it to heart!

Karma: The Law of Cause and Effect

The third of the four mind-changings has to do with the consequence of actions, the law of karma. This simply means that in our thoughts, in our words, and in our deeds, if we do evil, it has a negative consequence; it brings suffering and pain. If in our thoughts, words, and deeds we do what is good and helpful, it brings happiness and well-being. It is as simple as that. That is the main principle of the karmic consequence of one's actions. What we do has a consequence that is unfailing; there is no mistake. Evil brings a result that is unpleasant. When doing good, it brings a pleasant result. There is no mistake in that. Therefore, it is very important that one doesn't confuse what needs to be rejected and what needs to be accepted in one's behavior. That is the very basis for all Dharma practice.

Defects of Samsara

The last of the four mind-changings is about the negative sides of samsara. In the three lower realms, among hell beings and hungry ghosts, there is nothing but suffering. Among animals, there are some pleasant moments, but not many. Mostly, animals eat one another and are in constant fear of being hunted down and killed by other animals. Human beings, Asuras, and Devas have more pleasure; but it is still a mixture with a painful quality to it.

Human beings suffer when they are born, when they age, when they fall sick, and when they die. But there are many other kinds of worries, especially of being unfulfilled, of having this sense of not yet having obtained what one needs. That itself is painful. We want so much. It doesn't happen the way we would like it to. We want what we want, and we want to avoid what is unpleasant, and yet it happens. That is painful. We have enemies, those people we don't get along with. There is disease, there is failure. We have intimates, our friends and relatives; we have the money we love and the things in our lives that are really dear to us. We don't want to part from all of that, and yet we will. We have to part from those things, temporarily as well as finally.

In each moment of conceptual thought there is hope and fear. This hope and fear is agonizing, a very subtle pain. Based on that, there can be huge pain. Sometimes whole mountain ranges catch fire, although the first cause might not have been more than someone throwing a match or a cigarette. It takes just a little bit to have a huge effect. In each moment of thought, if the subtle hope and fear that are present are allowed to take hold and be amplified in our minds, the misery can be horrible.

There are also the traditional ways of describing suffering: the suffering of change, the suffering upon suffering, and the all-pervasive suffering of being conditioned, along with many other details. Seen from the perspective of a completely enlightened Buddha, coming into being, being born, is painful. Living is painful; existing is painful. Falling sick is painful, and dying is painful. Birth, old age, sickness, and death are painful.

Samsaric states always have a certain negative quality. No matter where one is now, or where one ends up, in any situation within the three realms of samsara, there is no place that is of perfect happiness, joy, and pleasure. Why? Because all samsaric states are created through karma and disturbing emotions; all are conditioned. In any conditioned state there is no permanent happiness. Even though the higher realms are somewhat pleasant compared to the lower realms, none of that pleasure or happiness is ever perfect or lasting. There is no place that is truly beyond the three types of suffering.

When we really understand this, acutely, some disenchantment arises within us. We have developed some distaste for pursuing further conditioned states within samsara. That is all we need, and that is the job of the four mind-changings. When we are no longer so interested in pursuing samsara further, what will we pursue? What really matters is realizing the essential meaning. The importance of the four mind-changings is that they can turn our interest away from samsaric states and toward Dharma practice. They can also help us to be more compassionate toward others, and to turn and direct our mind toward realizing the essential truth, the natural state of mind. Even if we have recognized this state, the four mind-changings will help us to realize it more deeply. In this way, the four mind-changings are very valuable. We need to know what this value is, what the purpose is.

THE EXTRAORDINARY PRELIMINARIES

All the levels of instruction in Buddhist practice are beneficial, reasonable, and meaningful, and, when applied, they work. That goes for the common and the extraordinary preliminaries at the beginning, all the way up to, and including, the practices of Mahamudra and Dzogchen. All are equally beneficial; all are equally reasonable. In other words, they are meant to work, and they do work.

The extraordinary preliminaries, the *ngöndro,* involve purifying obscurations. They also involve how to perfect the accumulations in a way that is very simple, does not require much effort, and is extremely effective. They are renowned as the four times, or sometimes, five times a hundred thousand preliminaries. The preliminary practices consist of refuge and *bodhichitta,* Vajrasattva meditation, mandala offering, and guru yoga. The purification of obscurations is the way to remove unfavorable circumstances. Perfecting the accumulations is a way to provide favorable circumstances and conducive conditions.

REFUGE

The first of these preliminary practices is taking refuge and generating bodhichitta. Sometimes they are practiced in combination with bowing down, known as prostrating. In the past we have created an immense amount of negative karma with our physical bodies by taking others' lives and stealing their possessions, by sexual misconduct, and so forth. And we have created this not only by what we ourselves have actually done, but also by what we have incited or provoked others to do, or rejoiced in others doing. When we take refuge with the bodhisattva attitude and bow down a hundred thousand times in a very sincere, wholehearted way, all the negative karma created through our physical body can be purified. It is not only the negative karma from this lifetime that is purified, but also that from past lives. This is not a Tibetan invention; this is utilizing the intent explained in the tantras.

Someone who wants to be free of samsaric existence and is not able to do so through his or her own power seeks help by taking refuge in the Three Jewels: the Buddha, the Dharma, and the Sangha. The Buddha is someone who is totally free from what needs to be abandoned, all obscurations and so forth, and totally endowed with all perfect qualities, wisdom, love, capability. The instructions that we make use of to be free of karma and disturbing emotions are the sacred Dharma. We can receive these teachings from individuals who are part of the noble Sangha. Enlightenment itself is the state of Buddha. The Dharma is what we put to use, what we train in; the Sangha is our companions.

Taking refuge is something extremely important and very profound. In order to truly take refuge, or place one's trust in something, we need to know the qualities of those objects in which we place our trust. We need to understand that the real qualities of the Buddha, the Dharma, and the Sangha are authentic, beneficial, unfailing, and never deceiving. It is through taking the support of the Three Jewels that we are enabled to be liberated and enlightened. Without taking help from the Three Jewels, there is no real way to be free, to awaken to buddhahood. If there were some other way, of course it would be all right to use that. Please understand this; it is important.

The Three Jewels are the precious Buddha, the precious Dharma, and the precious Sangha. These are the three general objects of refuge, which are shared by all levels of Buddhism. According to Vajrayana, there are also the inner objects of refuge, which are the three roots. The guru is the root of blessings, the yidam is the root of accomplishment, and the dakinis and Dharma protectors are the root of activities that dispel obstacles. On an innermost level, the objects of refuge are the three kayas. In this way, there are the ninefold objects of refuge. They are counted as nine, but please understand that in reality they are indivisible.

Taking refuge has to do with entrusting oneself and seeking help, taking support. This is an act that is real; it is something authentic. It is thanks to the objects of refuge that we can progress through the stages that lead toward liberation and enlightenment. It is through the inconceivable qualities of the objects of refuge that our obstacles are removed, our hindrances overcome. The more we learn about the qualities that the objects of refuge contain, the more delight we can take in taking refuge. Taking refuge is something undeceiving and genuine; taking refuge moves us closer to being free and enlightened.

Among the Three Jewels, what is most important to us temporarily or immediately? It is our spiritual teacher, our guide. Also, it is the sacred Dharma, the teachings that we can apply in order to progress. But ultimately, the most important object of refuge is the Buddha.

What exactly is the Buddha? We can say there are two aspects: There is the symbolic Buddha, and there is the real Buddha. The symbolic Buddha is someone who took birth in Lumbini, approximately 2,500 years ago. He awakened to true and complete enlightenment at the Vajra Seat in Bodhgaya. He turned the wheel of Dharma in Varanasi and finally passed away in Kushinagar. That is what we call the symbolic Buddha; the fourth guide of this aeon. The real Buddha is the state that is totally free of all obscurations, in which all the qualities, the inconceivable, great qualities of wisdom, of compassion, of abilities are complete and perfected. In other words, wherever the state of being totally purified and totally perfected is present, that is the real Buddha. That is our ultimate object of refuge, and also the ultimate object of realization. In order to gain this realization, we need some method, and this method is taking the support of a spiritual teacher and of Dharma practice.

The Dharma is the path, and the spiritual teacher is our companion. The best kind of companion, the foremost spiritual guide, is someone who possesses an unbroken lineage. Why? Because, if the spiritual teacher possesses the living lineage, it is quite likely that he or she also has some blessings and some capacity. Why is the spiritual teacher so important for us on an immediate basis? It is because the words of the Buddha, and all the treatises by the great and learned masters of the past, are so extensive it is hard for anyone to extract what is important and what is applicable

for oneself at the present time. So the spiritual teacher is someone who can distill and present the vital points of the Dharma
practices and make them clear to us. Otherwise, we don't know
how to purify our obscurations and gain realization. It is through
the kindness of the spiritual teacher that we can understand the
intention of the Buddha's teaching. Someone who really understands can pass the message on to us, the message of the Buddha.
If we gain clarity about how to remove our obscurations, and how
to allow the realization to unfold, then we have received the message of the Buddha very correctly.

In Vajrayana, one considers one's personal master to be
extremely kind. There is a tremendous sense of gratitude involved
in that. This is hard to understand from the perspective of the
general teachings. In the general vehicles of Buddhism, you don't
think of the teacher as being a buddha. You don't have to. You
think of the teacher as being someone who is a very good person. The teacher is someone who keeps the Vinaya very purely,
who has practiced a great deal, become a capable meditator by
means of *shamatha* and *vipashyana,* and is qualified to be a guide
to others. As a spiritual guide, he or she is considered part of the
Sangha, not the Buddha.

In Vajrayana, the main emphasis is on pure perception. Vajrayana
is called taking pure perception as the path, using pure perception.
Toward one's guru, who is regarded as a buddha in person, one
cultivates pure perception. And not only toward the teacher, but
toward everything, including one's fellow practitioners. We have to
regard one another as on the way to being buddhas, whether someone is fully established on the path, or someone has put just one foot

on the path. We should regard our vajra brothers and sisters as yogis and *yoginis.* Some are pretty advanced already; some are close to being enlightened; some are just about to be enlightened; some may already be enlightened. Who knows? Really, who knows? Some of them may already be *siddhas,* accomplished beings. We should allow for that possibility and then have respect for one another.

Moreover, all other people, all other beings as well, possess buddha nature, and therefore have the potential, have a nature that is in fact already pure and waiting to be revealed. We should respect that in others as well and develop the kind of appreciation that regards everyone and everything as pure. This is especially so with respect to our teacher. In Vajrayana we need to have pure perception, because the teacher reveals the very intent of the tantras. It is the teacher who confers empowerment and who gives the pith instructions on how to realize to realize the nature of our mind. It is not only that someone teaches and explains; during that time we ourselves have a glimpse, and the realization dawns as to what the nature of mind, the buddha nature, really is.

There are different ways of explaining what a root guru is. According to some systems, the root guru is the one who gives empowerment, explains the tantras, and gives the pith instructions. At other times the root guru is regarded as the one who not only did that, but who personally pointed out and helped us recognize the nature of mind. In any case, it is someone we regard with extreme, deeply felt gratitude. Of course it is all right to say that the one who gave you all the empowerments and the pith instructions is your root guru, but the true root guru is the one who showed you the way to liberate your stream of being.

It is said that the person who introduces you to the ultimate intrinsic wakefulness, the state of realization, is equal in kindness or preciousness to the Buddha. But, personally, the kindness of such a person for oneself is even greater than the kindness of the Buddha. Why is that? Even if we met the Buddha in person, and received his teachings, the Buddha cannot do anything greater for us than to liberate our stream of being, through introducing us to the state of original wakefulness. Therefore, there is no difference whether it is done by the Buddha or by our personal root guru. In this way, the root guru and the Buddha are equally precious. In terms of kindness, our personal root guru is even more important. Why? Because we didn't meet the Buddha; we didn't have that karmic fortune—we were somewhere else. The one who appears to us in a human form and introduces us to the wisdom of realization, so that we recognize it, is, from our perspective, even more precious and kind than the Buddha himself. Another point to remember is that all the blessings of the lineage from the Buddha, the bodhisattvas, and all the lineage gurus have been passed down to and are embodied in our root guru.

To reiterate, the Buddha means the perfection of the qualities of abandonment and realization. The Dharma is the path, the remedy against disturbing emotions. The Sangha is of various types. The supreme noble Sangha is the great beings on the various levels of enlightenment, the bhumis, and also the arhats, and so forth. Then there is the ordained Sangha, sometimes called the ordained noble Sangha. This means those who wear the triple robes and have shaved heads and so forth. There is also the Sangha of ordinary beings, but remember, we don't always know who is an ordinary being and who isn't. It could be that there are members of the noble Sangha among the ordinary beings.

The next point to consider is the inner objects of refuge: the guru, yidam, and dakini. I have already explained quite a bit about the guru. The second of the three roots is the yidam. The yidam is the form of a buddha with whom we have a particular karmic link, and is dependent upon our present inclination, disposition, abilities, faculties, interest, and so forth. Through that yidam, we will have a quicker way to purify what needs to be purified and realize what needs to be realized. The third root is the dakinis and Dharma protectors who are already enlightened, who have already abandoned, perfected, and realized. But they still take a form to remove obstacles and to assist and accompany practitioners on the path.

Finally, the innermost refuge is the three kayas. They can be described in different ways. Sometimes the dharmakaya buddha is Samantabhadra; sometimes it is Vajradhara. The sambhogakaya includes the five buddha families; the nirmanakaya is Buddha Shakyamuni. Sometimes the dharmakaya is Amitabha, the sambhogakaya is Avalokiteshvara, and the nirmanakaya is Padmasambhava. There are various ways to describe the representations of the three kayas.

The nine aspects that have been described, the Buddha, Dharma, Sangha, guru, yidam, dakini, and the three kayas, are called the ninefold objects of refuge. Whichever ngöndro we prefer to practice should always be done by embracing all the practices with the attitude of refuge and bodhichitta. Whether we are bowing down, reciting the mantra of Vajrasattva, making mandala offerings, or practicing guru yoga, we should always do so while embracing those practices with the attitude of refuge and bodhichitta. We should always conclude with dedication and making pure aspirations. In this way, the ngöndro is a way of using the threefold excellences.

BODHICHITTA

Bodhichitta attitude means to train in a way that doesn't aim at liberation and enlightenment for yourself alone, or for you and your friend, or for those you love. It is a vaster, more encompassing frame of mind that includes all sentient beings, infinite in number, in one's practice. This attitude of bodhichitta is very profound, very precious, very pure. Whatever spiritual practice we do has a tremendous effect when we are motivated by that attitude of bodhichitta.

If possible, we should embrace this bodhichitta attitude with the three powers: the power of wisdom, the power of knowledge, and the power of dedication. The power of wisdom is to not fixate on concepts of subject, object, and action. A lot could be explained about the power of wisdom, of not holding onto the threefold concepts. One perspective is that it means understanding that everything is like magic. When giving, the object we give is just like a magical apparition. You, the giver, are also like magic. The act of giving is also just like a magical apparition; it is insubstantial.

The power of knowledge is more in the sense of intelligence, of pure understanding, in how we direct ourselves: not aiming at a result that is of personal benefit, such as making ourselves famous, rich, beautiful, healthy, and so forth; also, not aiming at attaining some luxurious, beautiful, pleasant state in the next life—not aiming at any such samsaric conditioned state. That is the power of knowledge.

The power of dedication is different from the way an ordinary person conceptually shares goodness or directs the outcome of an action. It is making the wish that the goodness created throughout past, present, and future may be shared with all sentient beings, infinite in number. We try to do this in exactly the same way as the buddhas and their sons and daughters of the three times and ten directions do. It is a special quality of Mahayana practice that any spiritual practice we do, even a tiny one, which is embraced with the three powers, becomes immense, tremendous.

Prostrations

The way to take refuge and combine that with prostrations is as follows. The prayer that is chanted depends on which ngöndro you are doing. Sometimes it is refuge by itself, sometimes refuge together with bodhichitta. But the visualization is basically like this. You are in a place that is inconceivably vast and open. The earth is level, and it is a beautiful place. In the center of this land there is a lake that is of the clearest, cleanest, nicest water, all the best properties of water. Here grows a huge wish-fulfilling tree that has one trunk and five branches, one in each of the cardinal directions and one that grows straight up. On the middle branch sits the central object of refuge. This central figure could be Buddha Vajradhara, Padmasambhava, or the like, depending on which ngöndro you use. Please understand that this figure is the embodiment of all enlightened beings as one, and his mind is not different from the realized mind of your own personal root guru. To his right side is a branch with all the buddhas of the three times and ten directions, surrounding Buddha Shakyamuni. To his left side is the enlightened Sangha, the bodhisattvas of the greater vehicle, Mahayana, and the liberated *shravakas* and *pratyekabuddhas* of the lesser vehicle, Hinayana. Behind him are all the scriptures of the three vehicles written in pure gold on pages of lapis lazuli. All the teachings are resounding, by themselves, from these pages. In front of him, on the fifth branch, are all the yidams of all the six sections of tantra.

When you imagine all the objects of refuge in the refuge tree, you should think of them as being alive and vividly present, in a way which is distinct and unmixed. If you can, visualize their detailed features, including the very eyelashes and the white and black parts of their eyes. All the objects of refuge are looking at you with open eyes, loving, wise, and capable. They are extending their blessings to all beings, guiding them until complete enlightenment.

Who is taking refuge here? It is mainly yourself. You are the chief figure on the bank of this lake, surrounded by all other beings, present in an extremely large number. All beings are there, with your father on your right side, your mother on your left side, and all your other fathers and mothers of past lives extending out into all directions. You are chanting together, with you as lead chanter, and you are all bowing down together. When you prostrate, think of the kindness of the guru who bestowed the instructions upon you.

When bowing down, you first join the palms of your hands as a beautiful lotus bud. Touch the crown of your head, while wishing that all the negative karma from all past lives be purified. When you move the hands up to your forehead, bring to mind the negative actions created by the physical body, not just by yourself, but by all sentient beings as well. Remember all the killing, all the stealing, all the sexual misconduct, that you have personally done, induced others to do, or rejoiced in others doing, either directly, indirectly, or implicitly. Think, "I apologize; I deeply apologize. Please forgive all of this; please let it be purified. Please bestow your blessings to realize the body of all the conquerors, realizing that all sights are visible emptiness."

You then move the hands down to your throat, while wishing that all negative actions created through your voice be purified. Bring to mind all the negative actions committed through speech: the lying, harsh words, divisive talk, idle gossip, whether committed directly, indirectly, implicitly, by yourself, by all others, and in all lifetimes, including this one. With remorse, apologize for that and ask for the blessings to realize the voice of all the conquerors, which is audible emptiness.

Then you touch your heart and wish that all negative thoughts and attitudes be purified. Bring to mind the negative actions and obscurations created throughout all lifetimes, through forming ill will, craving, and harboring wrong views, by yourself and by all others. Ask for the blessings to realize the mind of all buddhas, the awakened state, the view of Mahamudra and Dzogchen, not at some time in the future, but at this very moment. Make the wish to receive the blessings, the accomplishments, and the empowerments of enlightened body, speech, and mind; visible emptiness, audible emptiness, and aware emptiness.

Next, place the five points of your body—forehead, two hands, and two knees—on the ground and make the wish that the five poisons, the five disturbing emotions, be purified, and that the five wisdoms be realized. You stand up again, in a way that is not rushed, not too slow or lazy, a balanced pace. That is one prostration. We do one hundred thousand of these prostrations in a very sincere, balanced way, and that is the way of combining refuge with prostrations. While doing so, we should not let our attention stray toward anything else, but continually practice in a way that is delighted and joyful.

One more point about prostrations is that there is a reason for prostrating, for bowing oneself to the floor. The reason is that our head is the highest point in our body, while the earth on which we stand is the lowest. Putting our head down to that ground shows that we are bowing ourselves to something we consider greater or more important than ourselves. In other words, it is the deepest gesture of respect that a human being can make. Why do we do that? It is because we acknowledge that the objects of refuge are the embodiment of the highest qualities possible, of abandonment and realization. The objects of refuge represent those qualities we don't have yet, but want to have. We understand the value of those qualities and respect them. One is willing to surrender oneself to the realization of those qualities. There is nothing more respectful we can do with our body than to bow down. Therefore, one purpose of prostrating is to show respect. The second purpose is to reduce our pride, our conceit, the thinking of our deluded state as being great and important.

Concluding a Session

When we come to the end of the session, we imagine that all the objects of refuge send the blessings of their body, speech, and mind into ourselves. First they all dissolve into the central figure, so that there is Padmasambhava or Vajradhara left, who is the mind of your guru in the awakened state. At that time, imagine that because the Buddha, Dharma, and Sangha and the yidams, dakinis and Dharma protectors have all dissolved into the central figure, the majestic presence is even more resplendent and brilliant than before. Imagine that from his forehead, his throat, and his heart three rays of light simultaneously enter ourselves and we receive the four empowerments, the blessings of the body, speech, and mind. Finally, the central figure also dissolves into ourselves. Just like a snowflake dissolving into the surface of water, he dissolves into ourselves, and hereby we have absorbed all the objects of refuge. At that point, it is perfectly all right for you to imagine that you look just like Padmasambhava or Vajradhara; in Vajrayana, this is called "stable pride." You have purified the four obscurations, received the four empowerments, and attained the four kayas. That is the physical aspect of the practice.

Mentally, at that point, we try to remain in "ordinary mind," untainted by thoughts of past, present, and future. This is according to the Mahamudra tradition; according to Dzogchen, it is called "naked awareness." We try not to be interrupted by any ordinary thought involvement. Even if we start to think of something, we don't accept and reject that; we let it dissolve again and remain in this way for as long as possible. Please understand that this training in present wakefulness is the way to accomplish the mind of the awakened ones. The visualization of oneself as Padmasambhava or Vajradhara is a way to accomplish the bodily form of the awakened one. The recitation is the way to accomplish the voice, the speech of the buddhas. When we come to the end of the session, before we start to get involved in this and that, in ordinary thoughts, we should immediately dedicate the merit for the benefit of all sentient beings. That is one session.

To go into a bit more detail, at the end of the practice, you should always remember the excellent conclusion of dedicating the merit and making aspirations. Dedicating means that there had to be something good created; for making aspirations, we don't have to have done something good; we can simply make aspirations. But to make a dedication, there has to be something to dedicate. In other words, first we do some practice, and then we dedicate it; we share the goodness of that for the welfare of all beings, after which we make aspirations, pure wishes.

That is the best way to seal the merit, and it has to be done fast, right at the end of the practice. Don't wait until some other time, because it could be that we get angry and spoil the whole thing. It has to be done before we interrupt our practice with some mundane state of mind. We need to be clever about it; the more clever the way we dedicate the merit, the more the profit, the higher the profit! The most advantageous way of dedicating the merit and sealing the goodness is to seal it with the absence of conceptualizing the three spheres of subject, object, and action. It means to simply suspend your state of mind into the natural state. If we are not able to do that, then we make an imitation of it by just thinking, "All that is done, all the goodness, everything is illusory like magic, like a dream." And then we make aspirations.

We dedicate it not only to our friends and those people we like. If we have enemies, we dedicate it to our enemies, as well as to all other sentient beings, to the infinite number of sentient beings. We seal again while making pure aspirations. It is possible we don't know how to make the purest form of aspiration. If that is the case, then just make this wish: "Just as all the bodhisattvas of the past made pure aspirations for the benefit of beings, may my aspirations emulate theirs; may they be exactly the same as theirs."

VAJRASATTVA MEDITATION AND RECITATION

The second of the preliminary practices is Vajrasattva meditation and recitation. The purpose of this is to purify the negative actions and obscurations created through using our voice. Vajrasattva meditation and recitation is praised as being the most eminent way of purifying adverse circumstances, negative obscurations, and misdeeds. The way to do this practice is to imagine that above the head of our ordinary form, a buddha is seated on a lotus and moon disc. He is Buddha Vajrasattva, who is the embodiment of the wisdom of all buddhas, in a single form. Vajrasattva is white, but of a brilliant, shining color. He has one face, two arms, and is adorned with the sambhogakaya ornaments and silken garments. His two legs are in vajra posture. In his right hand, he holds a golden vajra at the level of his heart, symbolizing the unity of awareness and emptiness. In the left hand, he holds a silver bell, supported on his thigh, symbolizing the unity of appearance and emptiness. Sometimes he is visualized with consort, sometimes as a single figure. We imagine Buddha Vajrasattva in a very alive, vivid, and clear way, seated within a sphere of rainbow circles and lights of different colors. He is brilliant; he is radiant; he has a totally pure-white color. He is endowed with wisdom, with loving kindness, with the capability to purify all negative karma and obscurations. Vajrasattva is radiant like a full moon, visible yet insubstantial, empty and hollow inside.

In the center of his body, at the level of the heart, there is a tiny moon disc, on top of which is a one-inch-high syllable HUNG of a beautiful, radiant white color. This syllable HUNG is surrounded by the mantra of Vajrasattva in one hundred syllables. We begin to recite this hundred-syllable mantra of Vajrasattva, while directing our attention toward our visualization of Vajrasattva, the mantra-HUNG syllable, and the mantra at his heart that spins around. The mantra starts to radiate infinite rays of light in all directions. As they extend infinitely in all directions, they take the shape of all wonderful things, such as the sixteen offering goddesses carrying everything that is beautiful, luxurious, and wonderful in samsara as well as in nirvana, the seven royal possessions, and all kinds of precious stones. They carry whatever is beautiful to see, to hear, to taste, to smell, to touch, and so forth. We offer all of that to the buddhas and the male and female bodhisattvas in all directions, in all times, in a boundless way. Light rays return with their blessings and dissolve into yourself.

At some point, we imagine that other rays of light extend into all worlds where there are sentient beings. These rays of light alleviate whatever problems or suffering sentient beings have, and give them whatever they need. Whoever is cold gets clothing, whoever is hungry gets food, whoever is thirsty gets water to drink, and so forth. Whatever any sentient being could possibly need or want, we just provide that, boundlessly. Imagining in that way is called fulfilling the twofold purpose: one by making offerings, the other by dispelling the suffering of all beings.

Next we imagine that all the rays of light return and get absorbed into the body, speech, and mind of Buddha Vajrasattva, above the crown of our head. Through this, his radiance, his color, his magnificence becomes even stronger than before, even more powerful than earlier.

As the light returns, Vajrasattva's radiance is greatly intensified. This radiance becomes liquid and starts to drip down, to flow down as a stream, from the heart center of Vajrasattva, through his body, and enters the top part of our own head. When it enters our body, we imagine that it is a pure, radiant, splendid liquid that totally washes away the effects of negative karmic actions of our body, speech, and mind that we have created throughout all past lives, as well as this one. It also clears away the broken precepts, as well as the diseases we may have, and the harmful influences from evil spirits, as well as the effects of broken promises and violations of *samaya,* damaged commitments of Vajrayana practice. All of that begins to leave our body, pressed out by the nectar, and leaves our body through, not only the lower openings, but every pore of the body. It starts to escape in various forms. For example, we can imagine liquid charcoal or rotten blood, pus, disgusting insects, and poisonous small animals. All of that continues to leave the body until there is not even a single remnant left behind; not even the smell is left. Now our body is immaculate and utterly pure inside. Just imagine all that while chanting the mantra.

At the end of the recitation period, we say a prayer to Vajrasattva, a supplication, according to the text we are following. Often this one appears: "Lord of beings, supreme refuge, most splendorous Buddha. The evil actions I did in the past were like taking poison. Now that I understand, I will not take poison anymore. I will restrain myself from creating more negative karma, creating negative effects through violating the samayas, and so forth. Please bestow your blessings to totally purify, without any exception, all my misdeeds, my infractions, disease, and so forth. Totally absolve me, make me completely pure of all the effects, of karmic effects, and so forth." We should imagine that Buddha Vajrasattva, with a smiling face, actually says, "Yes, son or daughter, you are now totally pure." Having said so, Vajrasattva dissolves into light and is absorbed into oneself. We imagine that we become Vajrasattva and look like Vajrasattva. For a while, we should rest in the state of either Mahamudra or Dzogchen. After that, dedicate the merit and make aspirations.

Refuge and prostrations are a very effective practice for purifying the karmic effects of physical actions, such as killing, stealing, and sexual misconduct, so that no remainder is left behind. Vajrasattva meditation and recitation practice is especially effective for purifying the negative actions of speech, which are lying, divisive talk, harsh words, and idle gossip. It is also very effective for purifying the violations and breaches of the samaya commitments.

Vajrasattva is the buddha whose special quality is of purification, and also, at the same time, is the lord of the hundred buddha families, the embodiment of a hundred buddha families in a single form. We visualize Buddha Vajrasattva. We ask for forgiveness and to be absolved of all the negative karma we have created through our voice: the lying, harsh words, divisive talk, idle gossip and so forth, as mentioned before. By the downpour and purification of nectar, we purify our being and then conclude by dedicating merit and making aspirations. Buddha Vajrasattva is effective for purifying not only negative karma and obscuration, but also for disease and different types of illness. Imagine that the downpour of the nectar especially purifies your particular illness, and you may possibly recover from it.

Mandala Offerings

The third preliminary practice is mandala offerings, of which there are three kinds: outer, inner, and innermost. The outer mandala offering is to offer the three realms with all the luxuries and splendors of gods and humans. The inner mandala offering is to offer the body, consisting of the aggregates, sense sources, and elements, all our virtues and goodness, and so forth. The innermost mandala offering is to offer the buddha nature, the mind of all the conquerors, the awakened state of ordinary mind. The ordinary mind here is the wakefulness in which emptiness and awareness are indivisible. When it comes to mental negative karma, such as craving, ill will, and harboring wrong views, the outer, inner, and innermost mandala offerings are extremely effective. They are also very effective for perfecting the accumulations and providing conducive circumstances.

The outer mandala offering is to give away all the wealth and beautiful things in the whole universe. Those to whom we give it are the same as the objects of refuge at the time of taking refuge, except that there is no tree. At this point we imagine that all the objects of refuge are seated on clouds of rainbow light. We offer the entire universe with all its abundance of wealth. That is called the outer mandala offering. The inner mandala offering is our own body, sense pleasures, enjoyments, and so forth. The innermost mandala offering is to remain free of any concepts of offering and recipient. In other words, staying in the view of Mahamudra and Dzogchen, in thought-free wakefulness, is the innermost offering.

These are three ways to deal with eliminating, so no trace is left, the three misdeeds of mind. Craving is based on some object outside that we long for. Ill will is based on "me," on me being hurt and wanting to retaliate. Wrong views are based on the concept of identity, in oneself and in things. The giving away of all things eliminates craving. Giving oneself and one's sense pleasures away eliminates ill will. When completely giving away all concepts, all duality, then there is no basis any longer for harboring any wrong views. The basis for wrong views has dissolved through this practice.

The training in mandala offerings involves reciting some short verses, depending on which ngöndro text we are using, combined with making the offering. At the end of a certain number of offerings, we imagine that all the objects of refuge gradually dissolve into the central figure, Padmasambhava or Vajradhara. We imagine that all the qualities of enlightened body, speech, and mind shine through the central figure towards ourselves. Lights shine from the white syllable mantra oм in his forehead, red syllable aн in the throat, and blue нung in the heart center. These lights enter ourselves and we become suffused with the qualities of enlightened body, speech, and mind. We also imagine that all our obscurations from our physical actions, from our words, from our thoughts, from all past lives and this life, are totally purified in this way. Then the central figure melts into ourselves. We are, in actuality, Buddha Vajradhara or Padmasambhava. Our bodily form is Vajradhara, our voice is Vajradhara, and our state of mind is Vajradhara, the state of Mahamudra, Dzogchen, thought-free wakefulness. We remain like that for a while, and then at the end, again, dedicate the merit and make pure aspirations. That is, in short, how to practice the mandala offerings.

Skillful Means

We need to deal with the disturbing emotions in our minds. For example, when facing the happiness, well-being, and prosperity of others, it makes us uncomfortable. We don't like it, because it is them and not us. That kind of envy creates problems. It is unsettling for the mind in which those emotions move. It creates competitiveness; it creates ill will. Out of that ill will, sooner or later we want to hurt and harm the others, simply because they have a better situation than ourselves. It also creates covetousness: "I want his or her prosperity to be mine; I can't stand it." Such emotions are more or less lined up to occupy an ordinary person's mind. They are called mind poisons, or toxic emotions.

The methods of offering the outer, inner, and innermost mandalas are skillful methods to deal with mind poisons. When we make the outer mandala offering, bringing to mind the three realms with all the prosperity of gods and humans, and mentally give it away to all the buddhas and bodhisattvas, in that same moment we relinquish our attachment to all those objects. And in that same moment, craving, covetousness, jealousy, competitiveness, and so forth no longer have any foothold. There is not only an ultimate long-term benefit, but also an immediate, tangible benefit. That is one of the skillful special qualities of Vajrayana practice.

The first emotion was craving or covetousness; the second is ill will. The basis for ill will is clinging to "me," the inability to just let go of the thought of "my welfare, what I need," and thoughts such as "What could harm me? This will hurt me. They hurt me; I must retaliate." It comes about because of thinking, "I am important; I am so special compared to anything other. I am something that needs to be safeguarded and held onto; I can't just let go of that." That kind of tendency is the very basis for ill will. Isn't it? Instead of continuing this attitude, we make an offering out of the body that we care for so sincerely, out of our enjoyments, meaning our ornaments, our clothes, whatever we think of as being very valuable and important to ourselves, as well as our prosperity, property, and possessions—everything. We bring to mind whatever we really care for and give it away to all the buddhas and bodhisattvas. That will surely reduce our ill will.

The buddhas and bodhisattvas in the ten directions have absolutely no need for our body, our enjoyments, and our possessions!

This is only a skillful practice. It is only to be carried out in our minds. We merely imagine that we give all this; we are not actually doing it physically. Otherwise, it would be very difficult, because people don't like to part with things that they feel close to. But they can still imagine that they do it. We are, therefore, able to offer all of these things if it is only in our minds. It still works. To do something that works and which is easy—that is called skillful means. If we actually had to give our bodies, our things that we treasure so dearly, it wouldn't be skillful. Why? Because we wouldn't do it! If we had to give our most treasured objects away, we wouldn't like to; we would shy away from such practice. We would hold back the best part and maybe give the inferior piece to all the buddhas. Or, in the best situation, we might part with something of little value, but never the best. Isn't that true? Skillful means, many methods.

Vajrayana is like that: it has many methods and these methods are very skillful. There are not one or two methods; there are numerous ways to accumulate merit and perfect the accumulations. There are many ways to purify the obscurations, not only one way, but many various ways. All of these are very effective; they don't require much hardship. They are also not very expensive. They don't cost a lot, yet they work; they can reach very deeply. This is one of the special qualities of Vajrayana.

For someone to practice skillful means, there is a quality that needs to be present, and that is to be open-minded and intelligent. One needs to have open-mindedness to trust that this works, to be willing to try it out and experience the impact, the value. One could also immediately be closed-minded and think, "How can it work? I am merely imagining this; it is not real." Then one will never really penetrate the practice. It is necessary to be open-minded and intelligent.

When someone is not very open-minded or, you could say, when the flow of thought is untamed and frivolous, it is very easy to think this and that, whatever one feels like, without really paying close attention. That kind of closed-mindedness will think, "What is the use? I don't understand. Not really offering one's body, one's possessions, just thinking it, imagining it, how could that be of any use?"

Therefore, take something in your hand, a flat plate. On top of that put heaps of grains, medicines, precious stones, and so forth. At the same time as actually putting something physical on a plate, also imagine offering the three realms, the luxuries of gods and humans, your own body, your possessions, and so forth. Actually trust that "I am offering all this, I am parting with it, I am giving it away." That really does perfect the accumulation of merit of the kind with reference point, with concepts.

The second of the two accumulations is called the accumulation of wisdom beyond concepts. What is that? That is to remain in the composure of original wakefulness, in which the three spheres of subject, object, and action are not conceptualized. If you really want to please all of the buddhas and bodhisattvas in the ten directions, you should let be in this state of composure. Recognize natural knowing as being buddha nature, as being dharmakaya, self-existing wakefulness—your basic nature. Because it is in that state that you are liberated, you are free of all kinds of delusion, of karma and emotions, and that is the highest offering. That is what really pleases the buddhas. That is also the highest attainment for yourself. That is called the true view, the perfect view, which is the perfection of the accumulation of wisdom beyond concepts.

Regarding the two obscurations, making an offering of the three realms, the universe, the beings, all luxuries, is the outer mandala offering, and helps reduce the emotional obscurations. Giving the inner mandala offering of one's body, enjoyments, and possessions also helps reduce the emotional obscurations. Remaining in the composure free of forming concepts of subject, object, and action purifies the cognitive obscuration, and is the accumulation of wisdom beyond concepts.

Guru Yoga

The final ngöndro practice is guru yoga. The word *guru,* which is Sanskrit, is "lama" in Tibetan and means several things. *La* means above, superior; *ma* means mother, compassion. "Superior" or "above" refers to superior knowledge, the higher insight. Literally, *guru* means heavy or loaded, as in heavy with the sublime qualities of knowledge resulting from learning, reflection, and meditation; with the capabilities of being able to explain, compose, and argue lucidly; as well as being wise, pure, and noble. "Higher" has to do with the most supreme, the most eminent, which is insight, and the most eminent insight is the knowledge of emptiness. This is the view itself. The kind of knowledge or insight that is the most supreme is *prajnaparamita,* transcendent knowledge, the knowledge that realizes egolessness. Why is that the most eminent? Because it is through such knowledge that the basis for samsara is eliminated, the stream of confused experience cut through. Therefore, the view of emptiness, the knowledge of egolessness, is the most eminent knowledge, the most eminent insight.

Ma has the connotation of mother, which means loving or compassionate. This compassion is not limited in any way, and is not for oneself, but unbound and all-embracing—not an ignorant compassion, but one that is indivisible from the wisdom of emptiness. In other words, the real meaning of *lama* in Tibetan is the state in which the view of emptiness and the unlimited compassion are indivisible. In other words, compassionate emptiness is the real guru. Honestly, the state in which such knowledge and compassion are indivisible is what all buddhas of past, present, and future have realized. Likewise it is the realization of all the masters in the lineage of transmission; every lineage master, including our own root guru, has realized this state of compassionate emptiness.

The next word, *yoga,* is also Sanskrit. It can be explained in various ways as well. But in this context, the Tibetan word *naljor* is used. *Nalma,* from which we get the first syllable *nal,* means the real, the true, that which is authentic, unmistaken, not false. If something is real, it is not false. One needs to know which is which. If you mistake the false as being the real, it could be a grave mistake. The real authenticity has to do with the qualities of your original state, of the nature of mind that must be realized. This is what is the authentic, genuine, real. *Jor* means the way of connecting with that. Connecting with what is authentic, genuine, and real is the meaning of the word *yoga* or *naljor.*

The real thing is what the guru has realized. We want to realize that in exactly the same way, not in some way that is only a fraction or smaller than that. Also, we don't need to realize the natural state in any greater way than the buddhas have—just exactly *as it is*. That means without tampering with it, without distorting it. Our natural state is the same as compassionate emptiness itself. Compassionate emptiness is our innate nature. Therefore, you can ultimately say that recognizing the nature of mind is the real guru yoga. The true guru is the state of compassionate emptiness. The one who symbolizes this, the symbolic guru, is a living person. It is by means of opening up to that image, to that symbol, that one can realize the real guru, which is compassionate emptiness within one's mind. How do we do that? By bringing our guru to mind and making supplications to him or her, in the outer way. The inner way is through recitation. The innermost way is by receiving the four empowerments and then, ultimately, by remaining in the state in which our minds are mingled indivisibly. Sometimes we find it easier to think of our guru as he or she actually looks, and sometimes not. In the latter case, the skillful method is to visualize a form, such as Padmasambhava, Vajradhara, or Shakyamuni, and to receive the four empowerments from that form.

As mentioned, guru yoga practice in the ngöndro is comprised of three steps: outer, inner, and innermost. The outer practice is by means of supplication. The inner practice is by means of recitation of the main mantra of the particular guru yoga practice. The innermost practice is by means of receiving the four empowerments, mingling the mind of yourself and the guru into one, and remaining in the state of Mahamudra and Dzogchen. This is the recognition of our innate nature; it is what all the masters of the lineage, have realized, and this is what all the buddhas of the ten directions realized in the past, realize at present, and will realize in the future. The practice of guru yoga is a way to directly and immediately transmit the state of realization of all enlightened beings into our own experience.

The great master Gampopa said, "Realization of your original mind, of innate coemergent wisdom, is not the product of a lot of learning. It is also not the outcome of diligence or perseverance. It comes about through the blessings and instructions of a qualified master." That which provokes or triggers the receiving of blessings is our trust, our devotion, and our pure perception. In a sutra, the Buddha is quoted as saying, "Ultimate truth is realized exclusively through devotion."

The power of trust, devotion, and pure perception is tremendous; it can really open up our minds. This is because of the sincerity of these emotions. When we trust sincerely and open up in pure perception and faith, it is a very clean state of mind, very, very pure. This is especially true if the feeling is so intense that the hairs of one's body stand on end and tears are in one's eyes. At that moment, one is very close to recognizing the naked state of mind; the innate nature is almost laid bare. That is the power of devotion and pure perception.

We combine this trust and devotion with supplication, with making prayers. This is directed to someone we know in person, someone we have decided we can really trust, or to a great master from the past, like Milarepa, Saraha, Gampopa, Padmasambhava. We can also supplicate any other of the great siddhas and learned, accomplished masters. We think about their enlightened qualities, the example of their life, and then we can open up more in that way. That is the outer way of guru yoga. It is a way of cultivating devotion and pure perception. The inner way is by recitation. The innermost way is receiving the four empowerments.

EMPOWERMENT

Please understand that already as we speak, right at this moment, our body, speech, and mind are by nature the three vajras, but we don't realize it. When the body is not realized to be a vajra body, it is seen as material. For example, right now we think we have a body of flesh and blood. The voice is not realized to be vajra speech, but ordinary utterance that appears and disappears. The mind is not realized to be vajra mind, unchanging wakefulness, but appears to be conceptual thinking that comes and goes, disturbing emotions, selfishness, and so forth. To be caught up in this impure way of seeing body, speech, and mind is to be involved in the creation of karma. The result of that is experienced in different situations. For example, when we have done something virtuous, we experience for a while the realms of gods and humans. When we run out of the effect of that, we again take rebirth in the lower realms among hell beings, hungry ghosts, and animals. It can go the other way as well, up and down, around and around; we circle. In fact, the word *samsara* means spinning or circling, and we have done so for such a long time, spinning around and around in samsara.

We need to acknowledge our real nature as being the three vajras. The way to do so, the profound skillful method of Vajrayana, is to receive empowerment. Our nature is primordially that of the

56

three vajras. However these have been obscured by our clinging to ordinary body, speech, and mind. Thus through the guru yoga, our ordinary body is empowered to be visible emptiness, as vajra body. Our ordinary speech is empowered to be audible emptiness, as vajra speech. Our ordinary deluded mind is empowered to be aware emptiness, as the vajra mind.

By the first of the four empowerments, the vase empowerment, our physical misdeeds and obscurations are purified and we are introduced to the fact of visible emptiness. We are being implanted with the seed for realizing this. In other words, we become inclined to manifest the nirmanakaya. Through the secret empowerment, all the impurities, misdeeds, and obscurations of our speech are purified, and we realize audible emptiness. We thus become inclined to realize the sambhogakaya. Through the third empowerment, which is called the wisdom-knowledge empowerment, all emotional obscurations are purified. When really receiving this empowerment, we can realize the dharmakaya. The fourth is called the precious word empowerment. It is the ultimate, the most eminent empowerment. It is the introduction to or the pointing out of the original state of purity, the cutting through, or original mind, coemergent wakefulness. Recognizing this, and training in it, is the ultimate training. Through this we can realize the state of complete enlightenment.

We imagine that we receive these empowerments in the form of colored lights. After that, we remain in a state in which the mind of the guru and our own mind are mingled indivisibly. That is the innermost guru yoga. At the end, we conclude by dedicating the merit and making pure aspirations.

CONCLUSION

Traditionally there is a way to focus on ngöndro practice where you don't do anything else. You set aside all other activities with the thought, "Now I will just do ngöndro for a couple of months." It is also totally okay to do preliminary practice in daily life. However, we are often busy. Sometimes we are very busy; other times we merely make excuses and are lazy. If this is the case, it can take many years to finish the preliminary practices. If you are really focused, you can complete the ngöndro in a few months. For that reason, retreat is important. But even if you are not able to stay in retreat, you can still do ngöndro practice.

When in retreat, practice is divided into certain periods, with a beginning and an end, a fixed time. Some people do six sessions a day, but you should do at least four sessions a day, two before noon and two after. The length of these practice sessions is an individual matter.

The ngöndro is called the preliminary practice, but honestly, it contains the main part of training itself. There is always a point in each of these practices when we try to dispense with all concepts and remain in the natural state. It is this way with refuge and with Vajrasattva practice. At the end of the session, after unifying with the state of Vajrasattva, we remain free of any fixation. Also, when offering the innermost mandala offering, that is the offering of releasing all concepts. Training in the natural state of mind is the guru yoga practice as well. Practicing ngöndro creates the circumstances to actualize this state of realization that is innately present, pure, and perfect. Many practitioners have done so in the past by these means. We are simply following in their footsteps; we are becoming one more practitioner who becomes realized through the preliminaries.

THE GREAT GATE

FOR ACCOMPLISHING SUPREME ENLIGHTENMENT, A GUIDEBOOK TO THE PRELIMINARY PRACTICES

OF LAMEY TUKDRUB BARCHEY KÜNSEL
(THE GURU'S HEART PRACTICE: DISPELLER OF ALL OBSTACLES)

CHOKLING DEWEY DORJE

INTRODUCTION

NAMO GURU PADMAKARAYA.

Cloud banks of the magical net of the wisdom of great
   bliss
Fully manifested as the essence of the Trikaya Guru,
Embodiment of all objects of refuge, Vajradhara of
   Uddiyana,
With your lineage of heart sons, bestow excellence.

I shall now teach the short and condensed guidebook
On the preliminary stages of gathering the accumulations
According to the *Guru Practice Dispeller of All Obstacles,*
The ultimate among all instructions.

The persons bestowed with excellent fortune who, at the time
of having obtained this precious, free and well-endowed human
form, wishes to attain the unified level of Vajradhara in this same
body and lifetime should apply the ultimate of the paths, the
blessed guru practice. This is of great importance.

There are innumerable traditions of guru practice according to the New and Old Schools, yet the Old School of the Early
Translations is especially outstanding because of six great qualities. It has three transmissions of the teachings: the long lineage
of *kahma,* the short lineage of terma, and the profound lineage
of pure visions. Also, it has the lineage of the prophesied transmission the lineage of the empowered aspiration, and the written

lineage of yellow parchment. It is thus made special due to possessing the six lineage traditions.

Within the profound terma lineage itself there exist numerous kinds, such as higher and lower ones. It is said:

Eastern termas are ripened, like a fruit.
Southern termas are concentrated, like a stem.
Western termas are radiant, like a lamp.
Northern termas are unfolded, like a lotus.
Central termas are firmly planted, like a root.

There are thus five basic kinds. Among these, this one belongs to the Eastern termas, the group of teachings that are ripened like a fruit.

The undisputed and timely incarnated great treasure revealer Orgyen Drodül Chokgyur Dechen Shikpo Lingpa, Trinley Drodül Tsal, discovered an ocean like amount of profound termas. They are linked with the scriptures of the lineage, proven through the logic of the power of fact, adorned with the experience of oral instructions, and imbued with the supreme warmth of wondrous blessings.

Among these, this terma was discovered when the lord treasure master was twenty years of age, on the tenth day of the waxing part of the ninth month in the Year of the Earth Monkey, from underneath the foot of the nine-faced Great Glorious Wrathful One at the rock of Danyi Khala Rong-go.

This *Lamely Tukdrub Barchey Künsel* (The Guru's Heart Practice: Dispeller of All Obstacles) is the heart essence of the glorious Knower of the Three Times and the most unique among all the termas buried under the soil in the land of Tibet. It is the entire essential meaning of the wonderful vast and profound instructions condensed into one. It is the ultimate experience of all the conquerors of the three times that has never before been proclaimed widely in the past on the surface of this earth. Like the great treasury of the universal ruler, it is totally devoid of any incompleteness in the methods for attaining the boundless supreme and common accomplishments. In order to guide the fortunate disciples quickly to liberation and the level of omniscience by means of this terma itself, there are three topics:

1. Creating confidence through the historical narration.
2. Ripening through the empowerments.
3. Freeing through the oral guidance.

HISTORICAL NARRATION

I shall now explain, according to the words of the terma root text *Sheldam Nyingjang Yizhin Norbu,* a little of the history in order to arouse certainty that the source is pure and trustworthy.

NAMO GURU. On the tenth day of the first winter month in the Year of the Male Earth Monkey, the great master from Uddiyana, Padmakara, possessing the nature of the vajra body, speech, mind, and wisdom of all the buddhas of the three times, was living in the auspicious and blessed place of Red Rock Dense Tamarisk Forest, the stronghold from where the wish-fulfilling holy Dharma originated. He was residing in the three-storied great Dharmachakra of Glorious Samye, in the middle room called Glowing Turquoise Face. By his radiantly smiling face and the majestic splendor of the marks and signs, his body outshone all that appears and exists. With a Brahma-like voice, his speech opened an infinite amount of doors to the Dharma. His mind, without moving from the uncompounded space of the primordially pure depth of clarity, was spontaneously accomplished in all the virtues of wisdom, compassion, and power. Thus, he was residing as the main glorious and great one of the whole of existence and peace.

At this time and occasion, his pure entourage of fortunate ones was as follows: the lord of knowledge, the Dharma king Trisong Deutsen; Shri Heruka, Namkhai Nyingpo; Manjushri Heruka, Sangye Yeshe; the Hayagriva siddha, Gyalwa Chog-yang; the one with the transmission of the four rivers of Secret Mantra, Bendey Drimey Dashar; the master in magic power, the translator from Langdro, Könchok Jungney; the sovereign of all *kilaya*-holders in Po and Kham, Dorje Dudjom Tsal; the one whose mind was equal to the master's, Nampar Nangdzey Vairotsana; the great incarnate bodhisattvas, the princes; and also I, the woman Yeshe Tsogyal, who was granted to be the vajra consort.

All of us prostrated and with a single voice said, "Please listen, great master! You are the embodied mystery of the body, speech, and mind of all the enlightened ones. You remain as the central figure in infinite mandalas. Without depending on other tantras, texts, and instructions, we request you to grant us, in the manner of definite advice, the tantra of unimpeded wisdom that spontaneously arises in your mind's realm of great luminosity."

When we thus requested, he answered with a joyful smile on his radiant face and in a voice melodious like Brahma's, "It is indeed good that you perceive and request in this way. All of you worthy ones, headed by the king, ask whatever you desire, and I shall teach you."

At that moment, we felt tremendous devotion, joy, and courage, and again requested, "Please listen, precious master! It is a great kindness that you are revealing your wisdom mind in bestowing on us this tantra of vajra words as advice of oral instruction. When obstacles arise for practitioners of Dharma both at present and in the future, what will dispel them? When trying to accomplish the siddhis, how will they be accomplished? By what means shall the paths be traversed?"

Thus we asked and Guru Rinpoche answered, "Although there will arise infinite different kinds of obstacles for those who try to practice the sacred Dharma correctly, the only method for dispelling them is supplication to the guru. Advice superior to this has not been taught, is not being taught, and will not be taught, even by all the buddhas of the three times. When the obstacles are dispelled, that itself will accomplish the siddhis. Based on that, the paths will also be traversed. It is therefore of great importance first of all to supplicate the guru in order to remove the outer, inner, and secret obstacles."

At this time and occasion, moved by the inconceivable power of previous pure karma and aspirations, Prince Yeshe Rölpa Tsal offered a huge golden mandala decorated with shining heaps of turquoise. He prostrated himself respectfully many times and said, "Please listen, great master! In general, it is certain that all ones' wishes are fulfilled through supplicating the guru, but since today we must make a prayer that condenses to the essence whatever may be desired, please teach us a special way of making supplication to yourself, Guru Rinpoche, in order to remove all the outer, inner, and secret obstacles."

Thus he requested, and Guru Rinpoche replied, "Excellent, excellent, prince! In general, the guru who shows the path is the activity of all the buddhas embodied in a single person. In particular, the guru who gives the instructions in Secret Mantra is even superior to the buddhas of the three times. If one lacks devotion to him, having only a mere platitude, then the root of Dharma has become rotten. Especially, the guru of all the practitioners of Dharma in the country of Tibet is essentially only I. I dwell inseparable from the mind of all the dharmakaya buddhas. I emanate and absorb all the sambhogakaya buddhas. Through showing myself in different ways, though being of one taste with the wisdom of all the nirmanakaya buddhas, I incarnated in order to tame this world in general and Tibet, the land of the red-faced ones, in particular.

"The noble beings—the Dharma king, the translators, and the panditas—now living in Tibet, as well as the holy beings— the doctrine holders of the future—who will appear as long as the teachings of the Buddha last, are merely the magical net of emanations who tame beings according to their needs and are displayed from the vast wisdom mind of myself, Padmakara. Therefore supplicate me constantly without ever forgetting, with the devotion to me as the nature of the entire refuge and the embodiment of all the root and lineage gurus. If you do not attain all the desired accomplishments, then I shall have deceived all the buddhas of the three times. Supplicate in this way, especially in order to remove all obstacles."

Having said this, he placed his right and left hands upon the heads of the king and myself. Touching foreheads with Prince Lhasey, he spoke these words with the vajra-like self-utterance of the voice of *dharmata: [*The supplication expressed here is the *Barchey Lamsel.]*

[Later] on this occasion, the king and his sons again offered a golden mandala, a garment of brocade, and a vast and unsurpassed feast offering, after which they said, "It is an extremely great kindness for you to bestow in such a marvelous and special manner this instruction in making supplication, this wondrous mystery unheard of in the past, by means of the creation of aspects and forms of yourself, Guru Rinpoche. Now please, think with great love towards us who are assembled here as well as all the future people of Tibet, and bestow on us in full completeness the entire sadhanas, activity practices, and feast offerings that will pacify all the temporary and ultimate obstacles and accomplish, according to one's wishes, the infinite kinds of supreme and common siddhis."

As they thus prayed, Guru Rinpoche in person miraculously displayed himself in the dress of the great Nangsi Zilnön, the supreme sovereign of all mandalas, the lord who permeates all buddha families, seated with the buddhas of sambhogakaya and dharmakaya above his head, and with the mandala circle of a palace with deities such as the twelve main aspects, and so forth, around him in all directions. In the lapse of a single moment, he conferred the empowerments and taught an infinite number of detailed and condensed root instructions in accordance with the capacities of the fortunate disciples. Following this, the entire mandala circle was absorbed again into the Guru himself. He then remained evenly in the immortal vajra *samadhi* of immovable wisdom mind, the inconceivable state of the mysteries of body, speech, and mind.

These profound and extensive instructions are arranged in four major sets of teaching. The history has been narrated here to create a joyful inspiration. One should then be ripened by means of the extensive, medium, or condensed root empowerments, as well as by the subsidiary empowerments, and be freed by means of oral guidance for which there is the respective root and subsidiary, and guidance texts. In this root text there are the preliminary, main, and concluding sections.

The Preliminaries

First, the preliminary steps: These are in two parts, the preliminary for engaging in the session and the preliminary practices for becoming a suitable vessel for the path.

1. *The preliminaries of the session*

In a secluded place, sit with upright body posture on a comfortable seat and let your mind relax in its natural state. By exhaling the stale breath three times, imagine that all misdeeds and obscurations are purified. Think, "I will practice this profound path for the benefit of all the sentient beings pervading space." Then, above your head or in the sky before you, visualize your kind root guru, inseparable from Padma Tötreng Tsal, as the embodied essence of all objects of refuge. With immense faith and devotion recite this supplication, totally abandoning all other hopes: "Essence of all the buddhas of the three times, precious guru, think of me! Bestow blessings to ripen and free my being!" Recite this as many times as you can. At the end, imagine that the guru melts into light and dissolves down through the crown of your head. Mingle your mind with his and rest in evenness. This should definitely be practiced at the beginning of all the sessions you do.

2. *The preliminaries for becoming a suitable vessel for the path*

> Having obtained the supreme freedoms and riches, and being
> weary of impermanence,
> With intense renunciation endeavor in accepting and
> rejecting what concerns cause and effect.

As said, there are the general and special preliminaries.

The Common Preliminaries

The common preliminaries have four parts. These are the contemplations on

1. The difficulty of finding the freedoms and favorable conditions.
2. The impermanence of life.
3. The cause and effect of karma.
4. The inherent faults of samsara.

1. The difficulty of finding the freedoms and favorable conditions
    These freedoms and favors arc very hard to find.
    If I do not take advantage of them now
    To accomplish the benefit of beings,
    Later on, how will I truly attain them?

Saying that, contemplate in the following way. In the *Oral Instruction Lamrim Yeshe Nyingpo,* we find these lines:

    This bodily support adorned with the perfect freedoms
        and riches,
    Like the *udumvara* flower, is extremely hard to find.
    If you skillfully take advantage of it,
    Then this find has great value, exceeding that of a wish-
        fulfilling gem.

As is said:

    To be a hell being, a hungry ghost, an animal,

A barbarian, a long-lived god,
To have wrong views, to be in a time devoid of buddhas,
And to be verbally inept; these are the eight unfree states.

The five favorable conditions from oneself are:

To be a human being, born in a central land, with the
senses intact,
To have a rightful livelihood, and to have faith in the right
objects.

The five favorable conditions from others are:

The Buddha appeared; he taught the Dharma;
The teachings remain; they are followed,
And there is kindness from others.

Thus they have been described. Also, Shantideva has said:

By conduct such as mine,
Even a human body will not be attained.
If a human body is not obtained,
There can be only misdeeds and no virtue.

As is said:

Like a turtle able to put its neck through the hole of a
yoke
Tossed about on the great ocean,
It is said in that way is a human form very hard to find.

Moreover, it is said that the number of hell beings is as many as dust motes on a great field. Hungry ghosts are as many as sand grains on the banks of the River Ganges. Animals are as many as the husks left over from grain thrashing. Demigods are as many as snowflakes in a blizzard. The number of gods and human beings are no more than the dust motes that rest upon a fingernail. In general, a bodily support in the higher realms is rare, but rarer yet is the free and well-favored human body. The essence of this support is comprised of the eight freedoms that are the opposite of the eight unfree states. The five favorable conditions that arise from oneself are like an excellent figure. The five favorable conditions that arise from others are like the difference made by sunlight illuminating this figure. These are the special qualities, the ten favorable conditions. Whether one contemplates this precious human body endowed with the eighteen free and well-favored qualities through its cause, example, or number, it is extremely difficult to obtain.

One should form the thought: "If I do not practice a true teaching for attaining the unexcelled and permanent happiness now that I have obtained such a great advantage, it will be hard to find such freedom in the future. If I am reborn in one of the lower realms, there will be no thought of Dharma. Being ignorant of what should be adopted and given up, I will fall into the endless lower realms. I will therefore exert myself from this moment." Thinking thus, contemplate again and again through embracing the practice with the threefold excellence: the preparation of arousing bodhichitta, the main part free of concepts, and the conclusion of dedication. This should definitely be taken to heart.

2. *The impermanence of life*

> The three worlds are impermanent like the clouds of
>   autumn.
> The births and deaths of beings are like watching a dance.
> The life span of people is like a flash of lightning in the sky,
> And like a waterfall, it is quickly gone.

Say that. The *Letter of Dispelling Sorrow* mentions:

> On this earth or even in the higher realms,
> Have you ever seen or heard about
> Someone once born who would not die,
> Or do you ever have any doubt about it?

Also, Lord Nagarjuna has said:

> Since this life has many dangers
> And is even more transient than a bubble blown by the
>   wind,
> What a wonder that we have the chance to live on
> Between the inhalation and exhalation of a breath or a
>   sleep.

Moreover, the outer universal vessel with its four continents, Mount Sumeru, the god realms, and the surrounding wall, is hard and solid and remains for aeons, yet it is all also impermanent. There will be not even ashes left behind when seven suns and one body of water finally destroy all. Also, as to the inner contents of sentient beings, there is not a single one who, once having taken birth, will escape alive. You yourself will therefore definitely die. Not only that, but there is no certainty that you will not die tonight or tomorrow, or even right now between the inhalation and exhalation of a breath. The Lord of Death is coming closer and closer just like the shadows of the setting sun, and there is no certainty that you will die at a particular time and place. The experiences of this life are like the flickering of lightning in the sky, not lasting longer than an instant. For these reasons, it is most important not to let your Dharma practice slip into laziness and procrastination.

At the time of death, the true Dharma and nothing else whatsoever is of any benefit. Therefore you should contemplate again and again until you have taken this to heart and do not regard as permanent that which is impermanent, such as the outer world, its inhabitants within, the days and the months, and so forth. Padampa has said:

Once impermanence has been taken to heart,
First, it causes you to enter Dharma practice.
Secondly, it becomes a spur to endeavor.
Finally, it makes you attain the luminous dharmakaya.

Consequently, if you do not assimilate a genuine thought of impermanence into your being, you will in the end become nothing other than a "Dharma demon," no matter how many Dharma teachings you appear to have received and practiced. As Padampa said:

Of the Tibetan Dharma practitioners, there does not seem to be even a single one who thinks he is going to die. Still, I do not see a single one who will be left behind without dying. By their delight in wearing golden garments and gathering wealth, one thinks, 'I wonder if that food and wealth is to bribe the Lord of Death?' By the way they are piling it up, one thinks, 'I wonder if that is to bribe themselves out of the hells?' How funny to see these Tibetan practitioners. Ha ha! The least learned is the most proud. The best meditator hoards food and wealth. The one staying in solitude has the most distractions. The one who renounced his homeland has no sense of shame. These people delight in misdeeds. The fault lies in not acknowledging that one will die even when seeing the death of another person.

As he thus said, cultivating the thought of impermanence therefore opens the door to the preliminaries for everyone who practices the Dharma. For this reason, you should exert yourself, by all means, following in the footsteps of the holy forefathers by contemplating and practicing in this way until a genuine feeling of impermanence has truly taken birth in your mind.

3. Contemplating the cause and effect of karma.

    When, with the approach of time, the king passes away,
    His wealth, wife, and relatives do not accompany him.
    No matter from where to where beings may journey,
    Their karma follows them like a shadow.

You should chant those lines. In the *Sutra of One Hundred Karmas,* it is said:

The karmas of all creatures
Are not lost even in one hundred aeons.
When gathered and the time has come,
They will be ripened into fruition.

In the same sutra, it is also stated:

The joys and sorrows of all creatures
Are said by Shakyamuni to be karmas.
The karmas are innumerable,
And so beings act in various ways.
They wander and take birth in manifold ways.
This network of karma is immense.

No matter how much power and influence, wealth and enjoyment you may possess right now, when the time of death comes, the white and black actions you have gathered will, in spite of your death, not disappear. Thus you will be accompanied only by your karma. Through its power, you will be thrown either into the higher or lower realms of samsara to experience the inconceivable amount of different kinds of joys and sorrows. These all result directly from your own ineradicable virtuous and evil actions accumulated in the past. For example, as long as a bird is flying in the sky, its shadow is not apparently visible. It is not without a shadow, however, because wherever it finally lands, the totally dark shadow will appear. Likewise, although past virtuous and evil actions are not visible at present, there is no way to avoid their result returning to oneself in the end. Whatever virtuous or evil action we perform right now will ripen in the next life, or in the following one, and so forth. It is therefore most important always to arouse confidence in the truth of cause and effect. Do not belittle cause and effect with Dharma words of high views. For instance it is said:

Although the view is higher than the sky,
The cause and effect of actions are finer than flour.

In this way, it is vital to become more careful concerning cause and effect the more you realize the view, the meaning of the natural state. Consequently, at all times and in all circumstances, apply a careful scrutiny to your own mind by being alert and conscientious. Make a main point of adopting and rejecting what should be done concerning cause and effect, and do not let your view and action become separated.

4. Contemplating the inherent faults of samsara.
The three worlds blaze with the miseries of old age and
 death.
Consumed by the flames of death, they have no protector.
Samsaric beings are constantly deluded
And circle around like a bee trapped in a vase.

Chant those lines. Lord Nagarjuna has said:

Even if you roll the entire earth into pills the size of
 juniper berries,
It would not suffice to equal the number of one's past mothers.

In this way, although you have obtained the freedoms and favorable conditions that are difficult to find, you are subject to impermanence and death. You do not have the leisure to remain for a long time. If dying were like a flame being extinguished or like water drying up, there would be nothing further than that. But you do not vanish after dying; you must take birth again. As long as you continue taking rebirth, you have not transcended the realms of samsara.

In general, *samsara* or "cyclic existence" means that you circle around as on a potter's wheel, on the rim of a waterwheel, or as a bee inside a vase. A bee trapped inside a vase where the lid is sealed cannot go elsewhere but inside the vase, no matter where it flies. Likewise, no matter in which realm of samsara, high or low, you are reborn, you are not beyond the world of cyclic existence. The upper part of the vase is like the realms of the gods and humans, the higher realms, and the lower part is like the three unfortunate lower realms. In that way, the six kinds of beings circle around, being reborn in one realm after another due to the causes of conditioned virtuous and unvirtuous actions. Therefore it is called cyclic existence, samsara.

All of us have, since beginningless time, wandered through this samsaric world, and of all the sentient beings, there is not a single one who has not been our father or mother, friend, enemy, or neutral. The sutras say that it is impossible to count the number in the series of mothers of one sentient being, saying, "This is the mother of such and such." Although all samsaric pleasures at present seem to be happiness, they are in fact only causes that will ripen into the effects of misery in the future. For example, a poisonous tree with beautiful flowers and excellent colors appears to have delicious fruits, but if we eat them, they cause us to die of poisoning. For this reason, wherever you are born, in whichever realm of samsara, from the summit of existence down to the lowest hell, you will experience only suffering.

The three lower realms are the suffering upon suffering. The three higher realms are the suffering of change, and the perpetuating aggregates are not beyond being anything else than the all-pervasive suffering of being conditioned. Samsara, which possesses the nature of suffering, comes from the cause and effect of karma and negative emotions. Even though you are reborn in one of the happy states of existence due to conditioned virtue, you will still circle around to the lower realms again.

Through evil actions, you are tormented in the three lower realms. For example, since all actions other than practicing the true Dharma become futile activity and the nature of suffering, samsaric existence is like a nest of poisonous snakes or a pit of fire. Thinking that, motivate yourself with a strong feeling of weariness. Develop the renunciation of wishing to be free from samsara and the attitude of wishing to attain enlightenment. Feel confidence in cause and effect, abandon the concerns of this life, and feel love and compassion for sentient beings. These comprise the foundation for all the good qualities of the path. You should practice until they have taken birth in your being. For this reason it is necessary to contemplate these four mind-changings until you have taken them truly to heart.

The Extraordinary Preliminaries

Secondly, the extraordinary preliminaries have two parts, the general and the specific.

> The person possessing faith and compassion
> Who wishes to attain the supreme and common siddhis in
>   this very life,
> Should ripen his being through empowerment, and with
>   totally pure samaya.

Thus there are four parts: faith, compassion, empowerment, and samaya.

Faith

Generally, taking refuge opens the door to all the teachings and faith opens a person up for taking refuge. It is therefore essential to possess firm faith when taking refuge and when receiving teachings from a master or spiritual friend.

There are three kinds of faith that are called enthusiastic, longing, and confident faith. When you feel inspired and give rise to faith, due to circumstances such as entering a shrine room with many representations of the body, speech, and mind of the conquerors; meeting with holy persons, masters, and spiritual friends; and hearing about their good qualities and life examples, that is called enthusiastic faith. To wish to be free from the miseries of the three lower realms of samsara, to wish to attain the happiness of the higher realms, to wish to practice when hearing the good qualities of virtue, and to wish to abandon evil actions when seeing their faults; all these are longing faith. When you know about the extraordinary qualities and blessings of the Three Precious Jewels and of the masters, spiritual friends, and holy beings, and have confidence in them from the core of your heart, possessing at all times and in all circumstances the faith of total confidence, without any other sources of hope and trust besides the thought, "Everything is up to you, unfailing Precious Ones," that is called confident faith.

Orgyen Rinpoche has said:

> For male and female people endowed with faith,
> Padmakara has not gone anywhere, but rests at their door.
> In my life there is neither passing away nor death;
> There is a Padmakara in front of each devoted person.

If you truly possess confident faith in your being, you will receive the compassion of the buddhas wherever you are. Therefore, genuinely generating these three kinds of faith without letting them diminish due to circumstances is of great importance.

Compassion

In the *Sutra of Correctly Comprehending Dharmas,* it is stated:

> Do not train yourself in many qualities when desiring to attain enlightenment. Train yourself in one quality. What is it? It is compassion. The one with great compassion will possess all the enlightened qualities as in the palm of his hand.

The learned master Asanga has said:

> To not have the slightest faith even when seeing the
>   Buddha's qualities,
> To not have the slightest sadness even when seeing the
>   faults of samsara,
> To not have the slightest regret even when engrossed in
>   evil actions,
> To not have even the slightest modesty, shame, or
>   compassion;
> When these six shortcomings come together, there is no
>   fortune for enlightenment.

In the *Ornament of the Sutras,* it is stated:

> To precede an action with compassion,
> With devotion, and with patience,
> And to correctly apply oneself to the virtuous—
> These should be known as signs of a noble being.

For these reasons, the prime cause for the swift path depends exclusively on compassion. Exert yourself therefore in cultivating compassion. Direct your attention towards the miseries of all the sentient beings born as hell beings, hungry ghosts, and so forth. Keep the attitude that they are you and your parents. At the end, from the core of your heart, consider, "All these beings of the three worlds reach as far as the space extends, and evil karma and misery reaches as far as sentient beings extend. Poor beings that experience only evil karma and misery! How good it would be if they were all freed from the karmic perceptions, sufferings, and habitual patterns of each of the six realms, and if they would attain the perfectly enlightened state of permanent happiness!"

Then generate boundless compassion by thinking, "Just like my parents who produced this present body and cherished me, all of my parents in lifetimes since beginningless time are also kind beings who have cherished me in that same way. All of them are bewildered by the dense darkness of ignorance; they have lost their senses. Their minds are disturbed by negative emotions; they lack the eyes of knowledge to see what should be adopted and what should be avoided, and they do not have anyone to guide them as a spiritual friend. They lack the walking stick of merit to support their backs, and with their legs of method and knowledge broken, they wander through the lower realms. Due to the misery of karma, they have fallen into the abyss of the lower realms of samsara. If I were to abandon all these helpless sentient beings, who in this world would be more shameless and indecent? But what does it help just to say "poor ones"? I must guide them, my mothers, through various methods just like using a boat or rope to save someone who is being carried away by a river. I must establish all these beings in the totally liberated state of permanent happiness.

"Since I lack the ability to do that, I will seek the path of the profound and sacred Dharma in the presence of a qualified master, and having attained buddhahood, I will place all sentient beings in permanent happiness!" It is essential to assimilate an overwhelming compassion into your being, a compassion that is more than mere words.

Empowerment

The qualified master and spiritual friend is an actual guide for the path to emancipation and omniscience. You should therefore attend him respectfully. A master whom it is inappropriate to follow is described in the *Rangshar Tantra:*

> One who is ignorant and extremely proud,
> Who is deluded and pursues words,
> Without understanding the meaning of the Secret Mantra,
> Who hurts the heart of others, uses boastful words,
> And has entered a perverted path.
> One who has not had a vision of the mandala of
>   empowerment,
> And distorts the samayas,
> Who does not respond to questions,
> And has little learning and great arrogance;
> Such a master if not examined, is a demon for the disciple.

The great Master of Uddiyana has said:

> Not to examine the master is like drinking poison.
> Not to examine the disciple is like jumping into an abyss.

You should therefore carefully and correctly examine to see that he is endowed with the prescribed virtues. The characteristics of the master whom one should follow are stated in *Array of Ati:*

> To be learned and free from bustle,
> To have reached fullness in the meaning of dharmata,

And to be without ignorance in the desired teachings;
These are the characteristics of the Secret Mantra guru.

It is stated in the *Brilliant Expanse:*

Through the empowerment of a qualified master,
You will be liberated from misery.

The same text also says:

Having once obtained the empowerment to be a vajra
    master,
Act according to the words of the conquerors.
Scrutinize and comprehend the profound meaning,
And be free from the outer, inner, and secret distractions.

Be devoid of the faults of drowsiness and sloth, have high
    realization,
And confer empowerment with certainty and correctness.
Abandon the outer distraction of bustle,
The inner distraction of thought constructions,
And the secret distraction of a diffused view.

In general, you should follow someone who is learned in all the
sections of the Vajrayana tantras and who can distinguish the different philosophical views; one whose being has been ripened by
an uninterrupted stream of empowerment and who is free from
making conflicts between the samayas accepted in the empowerment and the vows; one whose being is peaceful and gentle due

to having few negative emotions and thoughts; one who has comprehended the entire tantric meaning of ground, path, and fruition in the Secret Mantra, Vajrayana; one who has had a vision of the yidam deity and perfected the signs of recitation practice; one who has freed his own being through realization of the natural state and who is able to ripen the minds of others through his great compassion; one who has abandoned worldly activities due to having given up the attachment to this life and who is focused on the Dharma with the exertion of accepting future lives; one whose heart is weary through seeing the misery of samsara and who encourages others similarly; one who is skilled in the methods of cherishing disciples by means of taming beings according to their needs and who possesses the blessings of the lineage because of fulfilling his guru's command.

Concerning the disciple, the one to receive teachings, it is stated in the *Rangshar Tantra:*

> The one without honor or respect,
> Who practices the Secret Mantra distortedly,
> Who has no dignity and no good disposition,
> Who is of little intelligence,
> Who disregards kindness,
> And who engages in futile and wanton actions;
> Such a disciple, when not examined, is the enemy of the
>   master.

In the *Brilliant Expanse,* it states:

> If the innermost essence of this *yana*

Is poured into those who are unsuitable vessels,
The vessel will break, the essence will spill, and they will
    fall into hell.

It is inappropriate to accept those who are not qualified, and it
causes the oath-holding dakinis to punish them. Then there will
be no accomplishment but only distorted understanding.

The characteristics of a disciple who is a suitable vessel are as
stated in the *Talgyur:*

Accept the one who has faith and great realization,
Who has interest and is free from delusions,
Who has clear faculties and attends his master,
Who has great faith and exertion in the view, meditation,
    and action,
Who is able to renounce and who respects his master,
Who is disciplined and who shuns misdeeds,
And who is unchanging and totally steady.

In the same text it states:

One who has the power of faith and is very diligent,
Who is highly intelligent and has no attachment,
Who is very reverent and who practices the Secret
    Mantra,
Who is undistracted in nonconceptual mind,
Who keeps the samayas and exerts himself in practice,
And who acts according to the word of his master.

As was thus described, [the students qualities are] to take great delight in and be deeply interested in the master and his oral instructions; to possess the enthusiastic, longing, and confident faith, the complete cause for receiving the blessing, which is perfect faith; to have established the resolve of fortitude that does not give in to postponement and laziness when accomplishing the unexcelled; to be able to realize easily the profound meaning of the natural state; to have little attachment to the joys and riches of samsaric life, such as food and clothing; to possess the gate for receiving the blessings due to highly revering the master and the supreme deity; to be able to engage in the profound practices by having resolved doubts and uncertainties about the path of the Secret Mantra; to be free from ordinary distractions such as passion, aggression, and delusion; to be without violations of the root and branch samayas; to be tireless and exuberant in the practice of the profound path; never to violate the master's word. A disciple who possesses these characteristics should be accepted as someone suitable to receive teaching.

The manner in which such a disciple should please his master is as stated in the *Brilliant Expanse:*

> One should offer what is valuable, children, wives, and
>   the splendor of wealth,
> What is highly treasured, and what is delightful.

As is mentioned in the *Rangshar Tantra:*

> The master who gives the oral instructions
> Should be served with one's body, with precious things,
> And with what is most unique.

You should in this way perform the pleasing actions of body, speech, and mind. The master should accept the disciples endowed with these qualifications through appropriate empowerments and key points of oral instructions in accordance with the degree of their intellectual capacities.

Without obtaining the empowerment that ripens one's being, one may not enter through the gate of the Secret Mantra. As is stated in the *Mahamudra Bindu:*

> There is no siddhi without obtaining empowerment,
> Just as no oil comes from pressing sand.
> When someone expounds the tantras and texts out of
>   arrogance
> Without having received empowerment,
> Both master and disciple will immediately after death
> Go to the hells even though siddhis were attained.

As it says in the *Shri Guhyagarbha:*

> Without pleasing the master
> And without having obtained the four empowerments,
> All those who listen and compose
> Will attain no results and will be destroyed.

The only entrance to the Vajrayana path is called empowerment. It is the special means of being authorized to practice the path and achieve the results. By means of it, the tantric view can dawn in one's being, one can meditate on its meaning, and obtain the ability to practice it. All the sadhanas, worship rituals, activities, mantras, and mudras will be meaningful, and one will have received entrance to the samayas. Since empowerment is like the source of all these, as well as the king that makes one attain the various levels, everything is based on it. For this reason, one should in this case first obtain the empowerments such as the extensive and medium root empowerments of *Lamey Tukdrub Barchey Künsel* and the four empowerments of the outer practice and guru service. In the *Root Tantra Embodying All Vidyadharas,* it states:

> By means of colored powder, mirror, and vase,
> *Torma* and various other articles,
> The guru possessing all the qualities
> Confers the blessing and empowerment;
> One will attain the four empowerments and the thatness
> of the fourth,
> The supreme essence of all mandalas.

According to the Early Translation School ["the Old School] there are the four circular empowerments, and according to the Later Translation Schools, [the "New School'] the blessing of Vajra Yogini. Having been ripened, the wisdoms of these empowerments are planted in one's being and one is able to engage in their practice.

Samaya

In the *Kündü,* it is stated:

> Having fully received all the empowerments,
> You should be careful to keep, without violation,

Any of the root and branch samayas.
Through that the supreme siddhi will be attained.

In a sutra it says:

When you abide in the samayas,
The foundation of all qualities,
That is the sacred life force of virtue,
Which matures into unexcelled enlightenment.

The tantric samayas or commitments are in brief included within the three categories of general, particular, and supreme samayas. The general samayas are the trainings of individual liberation, bodhisattva, and mantra. Although they are taught as the samayas of the outer tantras, they are not unnecessary or to be violated, because they are the foundation for the samayas of the unexcelled tantras. They are therefore called general samayas. The particular samayas are what is taught as the root and branch samayas proclaimed in the unexcelled tantras themselves. You should understand that the life force of these samayas is upheld through the view. They are not to abandon the unexcelled, to respect the master, not to interrupt the practice of mantra and mudra, to be affectionate towards the ones who have entered the true path, not to divulge the secret of the samayas of offerings, not to reject the five nectars, and so forth. The *Awesome Lightning* states:

Following this, the so-called samaya
Is taught to be one's own view.

The samaya is the source of all one needs, just like a wish-fulfilling gem, and it is like the life force of all virtuous faculties. One who violates his samaya is like a broken vessel; there is no way that the contents can remain inside. All his practice of the mantra path will be wasted. Since the samaya is like the earth, the basis for the qualities, it is the indispensable foundation for accomplishing the Dharma kingdom of all the great beings. Everyone should therefore hold it dearly. Here I have merely stated this in brief, whereas the details can be looked for in other tantras and scriptures.

Second: The Five Specific Practices

1. Taking refuge, the root of the path of liberation.
2. Arousing the mind towards supreme enlightenment, the essence of the path to omniscience.
3. Meditation and recitation of Vajrasattva, to purify adverse conditions, misdeeds, and obscurations.
4. Mandala offerings to increase favorable conditions and the two accumulations.
5. Meditation on the guru yoga of blessings, the root of the path of Vajrayana.

Taking refuge, the root of the path of liberation

From among these five, it is said:

> Taking refuge is the root of the path,
> And arousing the two types of bodhichitta is the essence of the path.
> The ultimate part of the path is Vajrayana.

Taking refuge is the root of all the paths. Due to the effects of virtuous actions such as the discipline of abandoning the ten nonvirtues, we may for some time be born in places of happy life-forms. If, however, we do not achieve the state of liberation where all misery is cast away, we will continue to wander endlessly in samsara and experience only a variety of sufferings. Indeed, we can be likened to a person on an island of cannibals, in a poison-ous lake, or surrounded by a burning forest. If we were someone who had gained independence and had no need to seek protection from anyone, then that would be sufficient. But this is not our case. Since beginningless lifetimes, we are suppressed by the deep darkness of ignorance, pierced by the weapons of karmas and disturbing emotions, and punished with old age, sickness, and degeneration. Finally, we are helplessly taken to the courtroom of the Lord of Death and sentenced to the three lower realms. The only ones who are able to protect us are the guru and the Three Jewels, no others. The Great Master has said:

> Samsaric masters, no matter how excellent or many, are
>   deceptive.
> The three precious objects of refuge are without
>   deception.

The *mahasiddha* Melong Dorje has said:

> Entrust always your mind, heart, and chest
> To the incomparable Precious Ones,
> And without fail, you will accomplish all your wishes.

Even all the mundane mighty gods such as Brahma and Indra do not have the power to save you from samsara. Just as criminals locked up in a prison cell are unable to help one another, the gods, also in samsara, cannot protect you.

Therefore, think, "It is surely only the Three Precious Jewels who are the helpers and refuge that can protect me from samsara." Letting your body and mind rest in naturalness, keep constant faith as described above, let the feeling of renunciation arise in your being, and contemplate the following visualization and attitude:

"This whole area where I am staying is a land made of all kinds of precious stones. It is even and smooth like the surface of a mirror, and free from hills and valleys, protrusions and depressions. This pure land with the perfect features of the Blissful Realm has lakes of nectar, wish-fulfilling trees, and flower groves filled everywhere with saffron and lotus blossoms. In the middle of a circular lake of nectar is a wish-fulfilling tree with five branches. Its luxuriant foliage and fruits extend in all directions, completely filling the expanse of sky to the east, south, north, and west. On all the minor branches are bells of precious metals; garlands of flowers; golden, intertwined ornaments; silken streamers of various colors; and pendants and networks of jeweled chains that, by the slightest breeze, proclaim the clear sounds of Dharma. These things are not material appearances of the nature of clinging to a concrete reality but are like rainbows and completely fill the entire extent of the sky."

Having envisioned this, imagine then as follows: Upon the slightly elevated central branch is a wide and lofty jeweled throne supported by eight gigantic lions. On this there is a seat of a lotus and sun and moon discs. Here sits the sovereign, the embodied essence of all the buddhas of the three times, my kind root guru who is a treasury of incomparable compassion. He is in the form of the Great Master of Uddiyana, Padmakara Tötreng Tsal, the Glorious Subjugator of Appearance and Existence. His body is white in color with a hue of red, and he has an expression of peacefully smiling wrath. He has one face and two arms. His right hand holds a five-pronged golden vajra, raised in the sky before him. In the left hand, he holds, in the gesture of equanimity, the *kapala* with the vase of potent elixir adorned with a wish-fulfilling gem and filled with the nectar of immortality. With his right leg bent and left leg extended, he is seated in the reveling royal posture. On his body he wears the secret white dress, the big blue gown, the upper red garment, the three Dharma robes, and finally the maroon brocade cloak, one on top of the other. On his head is the lotus crown that liberates by sight, marked with a golden vajra and ornamented with a vulture's feather at the top and with silken streamers and mirrors. In the crook of his left arm, he embraces his consort concealed in the form of a *khatvanga*. The khatvanga has three points, three heads one above the other, a vase, a crossed vajra, silken streamers, and bangles of tiny bells. His bodily form is seated in a sphere of dense masses of rainbow-colored lights.

Above his head is first the sambhogakaya Avalokiteshvara. He has one face and four arms, is white and radiant, and holds a jewel, a crystal rosary, and a white lotus flower. Above him is the lord of the family, the mighty Amitayus, who is of brilliant red color and holds a life vase in the gesture of equanimity. They both wear the sambhogakaya attire and are seated with their legs in vajra posture. All the masters of the mind lineage of the conquerors surround them.

In the area around these are the masters of the sign lineage of the *vidyadharas* and the masters of the hearing lineage of great individuals. Thus they are encircled by a gathering of millions of vidyadharas, gurus, and siddhas of the three lineages. They should be visualized as seated in tiers with the seat of the one above just barely not touching the head of the one below.

Upon lotuses with moon discs flanking the right and left of the throne are Mandarava to the right and Yeshe Tsogyal to the left. Mandarava is dressed in the attire of a goddess. With her two hands she holds an arrow with silk ribbons and the life vase. Yeshe Tsogyal is adorned with the red inner dress, a green upper garment, an orange silken scarf, and a head ornament with a turquoise crest; and her two hands hold skull cups. They both are seated in an affectionate manner.

Surrounding them you should visualize the masters of the special root lineage. First there is Nubchen Sangye Yeshe whose hair is in a topknot. He wears maroon clothing, and his right hand holds a vajra in stabbing position. The translator Gyalwa Chogyang, in the robes of a monk, has a club in his right hand, and a horse head neighs from the top of his head. The monk Namkhai Nyingpo holds a vajra and a bell in his two hands. Drimey Dashar, in the robes of a monk, wears the hat of the Tripitaka and holds a skull cup filled with nectar. Könchok Jungney, the translator of Langdro, wears monk's robes, a pandita hat, and holds a book.

The *tantrika* Dorje Dudjom wears the attire of a tantric practi-

tioner, a *raksha* rosary, and holds a kilaya dagger. The great translator Vairochana wears monk's robes, a pandita hat on his head,
and holds a book in his hands.

The Dharma king Trisong Deutsen is in royal robes. He has a
lotus flower with a sword and book upon it in his right hand, and
his left hand, in the gesture of equanimity, holds a wheel. Prince
Muney Tsenpo holds his right hand in the gesture of supreme
generosity and in his left hand, a white lotus flower. Prince Chökyi
Lodrö Murub Tsenpo holds a lotus with his hands in the wheel-
of-Dharma gesture, upon which is a sword and a book. Prince
Mutri Tsenpo holds in his hands a lotus, upon which is a vajra and
a bell. All three princes wear the royal garments. The great treasure revealer and king of Dharma, Chokgyur Lingpa, wears the
attire of a tantrika, the lotus crown, and a brocade cloak. His right
hand holds the stem of a lotus flower upon which there is a sword
and a book, and his left hand holds the life vase in the gesture of
equanimity. The omniscient Padma Do-ngak Lingpa is in monk
robes, and wears the pandita hat. His right hand holds a vajra and
life vase in the gesture of supreme generosity, and the left hand, in
equanimity, holds a white lotus upon which there is a sword and
a book. The incomparable Padma Tennyi Yungdrung Lingpa
wears the unfixed garments to tame beings through upholding
nonsectarian teachings, and his two hands hold a vajra and a bell.
All of these are to be visualized as a market gathering to the left,
right, and everywhere in between surrounding the supreme chief
figure Nangsi Zilnön Tsal.

On the branch situated in front of him is Bhagavan Vajrasattva
whose body color is white. He wears the attire of a peaceful divin-

ity and is seated with his legs in vajra posture, holding a vajra and a bell in his two hands. He is in union with the white Vajratopa who holds a knife and a skull cup. On the surrounding lotus petals, he is encircled by all the assemblies of mandala deities, the yidams connected with the six tantra sections of Kriya, Upa, Yoga, Maha, Anu, and Ati.

On the branch to his right is our teacher, the most compassionate Buddha Shakyamuni. His body is yellow like the color of refined gold. He has one face and two arms of which the right is in the earth-touching gesture and the left is in equanimity. He is adorned with the thirty-two major marks, such as the protuberance on his head and wheels on his feet. He is surrounded by all the buddhas of the ten directions and three times, such as the 1,002 enlightened ones of this Good Aeon.

On the branch to his back is the precious Dharma comprised of statements and realization. It is spontaneously manifest in the form of volumes with words, terms, and designations. They are of the red color of vajra speech, and with their silken title-flaps all facing myself, they are present in a splendid colored array, resounding with the spontaneous tones of the vowels and consonants.

On the branch to his left is the precious Sangha. The eight main bodhisattvas, including Manjushri, Vajrapani, and Avalokiteshvara, are surrounded by the sanghas of the greater and lesser vehicles, such as the noble sixteen arhats and the two supreme shravakas.

On the surrounding rings of petals are the glorious lords, the protectors and guardians of the Dharma, with the male classes facing outward and the female classes facing inward, performing the activity of preventing external adverse conditions and obstacles from entering and the internal accomplishments from slipping away.

All these figures are the wisdom display of the wheel ornamented with the inexhaustible body, speech, mind, qualities, and activities of the Precious Master of Uddiyana. These are the manifestations of the magical net of creations to tame whoever needs to be tamed.

In the presence of this resplendent mandala of the all-encompassing three roots and conquerors, for those who are taking refuge, you should imagine as follows: Your present father is to your right, and your mother is to your left. In front of you are your enemies, and behind you are your friends. In the surrounding area envision all the sentient beings of the three realms and six worlds, as numerous as dust motes on an enormous field, without any partiality concerning your friends, enemies, or neutral beings. Led by yourself, with respectful bodies, you all kneel down and join your palms. With respectful speech, you proclaim in a droning tone the lines of taking refuge. With respectful mind, you form this thought, "Whatever happens, such as being praised or dishonored, whether times are joyful or miserable, whether I have excellence, disaster, or sickness, I place my trust in no other than you, the Three Jewels and precious objects of refuge! Whatever happens is up to you! In whatever you do, please now consider myself and all sentient beings equal to the limits of the sky!" With the complete trust of thinking that, resolve to regard the guru as your guide, the yidam and buddhas as your teachers, the Dharma as your path, and the Sangha, dakinis, and Dharma protectors as your companions on the path. Keeping this attitude, with strong devotion and longing, recite once the *Sutra on the Recollection of the Three Jewels*. After that, imagine, "In the presence of all the objects of refuge present in the sky before me, I and all sentient beings take refuge with collective action of body, speech, and mind!" and say:

NAMO.
I and all the sentient beings equal to the sky
Take refuge in the Guru, Buddha, Dharma, and the
    Sangha,
Yidams, dakas, and dakinis, Dharma guardians,
And in all the ones possessing great compassion.

Count this up to a number such as one hundred, one thousand, or ten thousand in each session, and continue practicing it in sessions until you have reached one hundred thousand times of taking refuge. Accumulate the fixed and the additional thirty thousand, and continuously make the taking of refuge your main practice.

At the end of the session, imagine that your deeply felt devotion causes immeasurable rays of light to stream forth from the bodies of the gathering of divinities in the field of refuge. The light strikes yourself and all sentient beings, purifying all misdeeds and obscurations. Rays of light then stream forth from the body of the root guru striking the whole retinue of conquerors and their sons, whereby they melt into a mass of light and dissolve into the form of the root guru. He then glows immensely with brilliance even greater than before. Your root guru then melts into light and dissolves into you. Thus you rest evenly, as long as possible, free from the dualistic concepts of his mind and your mind, in the state of the great blissful simplicity. Afterwards, dedicate the virtue.

At all times and in all circumstances, never depart from being mindful, careful, and alert. Never separating yourself from the visualization of the objects of refuge, in all paths of action, such as walking and sitting, entrust your mind to the Three Jewels with total faith.

The things to abandon: Having taken refuge in the Buddha, one should not pay homage to mundane gods. Having taken refuge in the Dharma, one should give up harming sentient beings. Having taken refuge in the Sangha, one should not associate with heretical companions. Although there were no actual heretics in Tibet, one should not keep companionship with evildoers, those who slander the profound teachings of the Secret Mantra, or those who disparage one's master, since they are similar to heretics.

The things to adopt: Having taken refuge in the Buddha, one should not step on even the tiniest part of a broken image but give it immense respect and honor. Having taken refuge in the Dharma, one should not step on even the tiniest part of scripture but regard it as the actual Dharma of statements and realization. Having taken refuge in the Sangha, one should not depart from the notion that anyone who wears even the yellow robes is actually part of the Sangha of shravakas belonging to our Teacher, the Buddha. Moreover, when dressing in the morning, one should regard the upper garment as skillful means, the lower garment as knowledge, the sash as the unity of means of means and knowledge, and one's hat as the essence of the master.

Whatever action you are engaged in, you should never abandon the Three Precious Ones. Whenever you eat or drink, you should partake of it in the manner of making the first part an offering. When you are going upward, such as climbing a big mountain, think, "I am going to guide all sentient beings to the realm of great bliss." When you are going downward, think, "I am going to guide all sentient beings out of the lower realms." When going straight ahead, visualize the objects of refuge and think, "I am making circumambulations, accompanied by all sentient beings," and recite the formula of taking refuge. In short, as much as you can, try to embrace all the neutral actions that you do with the great intelligence of nonconceptual naturalness, to transform them into only positive actions of virtue.

The benefits of taking refuge in the Three Precious Jewels in this way are described in the *Stainless Sutra:*

> If the merit of taking refuge were to have a physical form,
> It would be even greater than filling the entire realm of
>   space.

This is also mentioned in the *Condensed Prajñaparamita:*

> If the merit of taking refuge were to have a physical form,
> Even the three realms would be too small a vessel.
> How can the treasure of water, the great ocean,
> Be measured with one's hand?

Furthermore it is stated in the *Sun Disc Sutra:*

The sentient being who takes refuge in the Buddha
Cannot be killed by ten million devils.
Although he may violate his discipline and have a
    troubled mind,
He will definitely go beyond transmigration.

As described in these and in other places, taking refuge has immeasurable benefits. You should therefore earnestly apply yourself to this practice of taking refuge, the foundation of all the teachings.

Arousing the mind towards supreme enlightenment,
the essence of the path to omniscience

This chapter has three parts:

1. Arousing the bodhichitta of aspiration.
2. Gathering the accumulations.
3. Training the mind in the bodhichitta of application.

Arousing the bodhichitta of aspiration

In order to arouse bodhichitta, the mind set upon supreme enlightenment that is the essence of the path, retain the previously visualized field of accumulation as a witness. While bringing the meaning to mind, think as follows: "Just as the truly perfected Buddhas of the past, along with all the sons of the conquerors, aroused the mind set upon supreme enlightenment and trained themselves in the disciplines of the bodhisattvas, thus will I also train for the sake of all my parents, sentient beings. They have again and again in my uncountable lifetimes been my father or mother, husband or wife, friend or relative. They have benefited me in immeasurable ways and have had the extreme kindness to protect me from numerous dangers. For the sake of all these beings, my old mothers, and motivated by great compassion, I will myself carry the burden of liberating them all from countless miseries. I will establish them temporarily in happiness and ultimately in the unexcelled bliss. In order to do this, I will accomplish total omniscience, the state of complete enlightenment!"

Thinking this, keep the bodhichitta of aspiration, the resolve to attain the fruition, chiefly in mind, and verbally say:

HOH
As all the conquerors and offspring of the past
Resolved to reach the unsurpassed, supreme
    enlightenment,
I will also reach the state of buddhahood
To benefit my mother beings, equal to the sky.

Whatever number you count to daily, such as ten thousand, accumulate in the end definitely one hundred thousand, as well as the extra thirty thousand.

Gathering the accumulations

For gathering the accumulations and resolving on the cause, arousing the supreme bodhichitta of application, there are two parts: preparation and main practice.

Preparation:
In order to purify your being and to perfect the accumulations, you should perfectly offer the seven condensed points of gath-

ering, purifying, and increasing. In the presence of the field of accumulation, the all-encompassing three roots, conquerors, and their sons who are manifest as filling the sky, you and all sentient beings should emanate as many bodies as there are dust motes on a plain and make prostrations with deep respect of body, speech, and mind. This is described in the *Sutra on Blossoming in the Direction of the Great Liberation:*

> Like the blossoming of a lotus flower,
> Join the palms of your hands above your head,
> And with cloud banks of innumerable bodies,
> Prostrate to the buddhas of the ten directions.

1. Prostrate with great respect of body, speech, and mind, and do not make mistakes out of disrespectful carelessness as to what should be adopted and what should be abandoned.
2. Symbolized by whatever you have in the way of material offerings, mentally create and visualize the offerings in the form of an inconceivably great cloud bank of offerings exemplified by the noble Samantabhadra.
3. Symbolized by the breaches of the seven kinds of vows of the *pratimokṣa,* the bodhisattva trainings, and the tantric samayas of the vidyadharas, as well as ordinary misdeeds, you should offer an apology with intense regret and remorse. Apologize for all your misdeeds, however many that you have accumulated throughout your lifetimes in beginningless samsara.
4. Happily and without envy, rejoice in the roots of virtue of all the noble ones, the hearers, solitary realizers, buddhas, and

bodhisattvas, and in all the meritorious actions performed by ordinary beings.

5. Request them to turn the wheel of Dharma in accordance with the different dispositions and capacities of beings, for the sake of saving the infinite amount of sentient beings from the ocean of misery.

6. Supplicate them for the sake of all beings not to let their form bodies pass into nirvana for many hundred thousand millions of aeons.

7. Symbolized by the roots of virtue gathered in this way, seal by completely dedicating all the virtues accumulated throughout the three times of samsara and nirvana to the cause of the great enlightenment. Then make prostrations while saying:

OM AH HUNG HRIH
I prostrate to Vidyadhara Padmakara
And to all objects of refuge in the ten directions.
I present you with a Samantabhadra offering cloud, filling
  the sky,
Of actual and mentally created offerings.

I apologize for transgressing and violating the
  pratimoksha vows,
The bodhisattva trainings, and the tantric samayas of the
  vidyadharas.
I rejoice in all the noble and ordinary beings
Who engage in the conduct of the sons of the conquerors.

Please turn the appropriate wheels of Dharma
To benefit the infinite number of suffering beings.

Without passing away, remain for the sake of beings
Throughout countless millions of aeons.

I dedicate all the virtues gathered in the three times
So that all beings may attain the essence of enlightenment.

Accumulate daily a suitable number, such as one hundred, one
thousand, or ten thousand. Cultivate the meaning until you finally
reach the number of one hundred thousand prostrations.

Main Practice

Second, training the mind in the bodhichitta of application,
the four immeasurables.

At the end, generate towards all these beings in the three realms,
the attitudes of

- The compassion of desiring them to be free from the cause
  of suffering.
- The loving kindness of desiring them to possess happiness
  and the cause of happiness.
- The sympathetic joy of desiring them not to be separated
  from the true happiness, which is devoid of misery.
- The impartiality that is free from prejudice, likes, and dislikes.

Form the thought, "In order to establish all sentient beings in
the unified level of Vajradhara, I will practice the profound paths
of development and completion in the Secret Mantra Vajrayana!"
and say:

By this merit, may all beings live in happiness.
Free of suffering, may it ripen upon me.
Never parting from the joy that is free of pain,
May they be impartial, in the nature of all things.

Recite this as many times as you can, maintaining the attitudes and visualizations, and repeatedly practice giving and taking by linking it to the inhalation and exhalation of your breath. At the end of the session, rest evenly in the state of not conceptualizing either the objects that give refuge, the person who is given refuge, or the attitude in between. Following that, dedicate the virtue.

All these parts comprise the general preliminaries of Mahayana and the common preliminaries of Vajrayana.

Vajrasattva

Among the special preliminaries of Vajrayana, the meditation and recitation of Vajrasattva comes first, especially to purify adverse conditions, misdeeds, and obscurations.

As is said:

All misdeeds and obscurations, the conditions averse to
    giving rise to experience and realization,
Should be purified through the profound practice of
    Vajrasattva.

Recite:

AH
Above my head, upon a lotus and a moon,

Is the wisdom form of all the buddhas,
Vajrasattva of the greatest bliss,
Stainless like the autumn moon when radiant.
Two hands are holding vajra and the bell,
Joyfully embracing Vajratopa, his own light.
Beautified with ornaments of jewels and of silk,
His two legs in the vajra posture,
He sits within a sphere of rainbow rays and lights.

Form this thought "That which hinders, obstructs, and harms our attainment of the precious state of the unexcelled and truly perfected enlightenment are our misdeeds and obscurations. Therefore they must be purified. The supreme method for purifying them is the meditation and recitation of Vajrasattva. I will make this my daily practice!" Let your body and mind then rest in naturalness.

With yourself in ordinary form, in the space about an arrow's length above your head, visualize a fully bloomed, thousand-petaled, white lotus. On it is a full-moon seat. Here sits the one whose essence is your root guru, in the form of Bhagavan Vajrasattva. His body color is white like a massive snow mountain struck by the light of one hundred thousand suns. He has one face and two hands. In the right he holds the five-pronged golden vajra of awareness-emptiness raised in the area of his heart center. With his left he supports the white silver bell of appearance-emptiness upon his thigh. His jet-black hair tied up in a topknot is ornamented with a precious band and a jewel crest. He is adorned by the five silken Dharma garments: the silk shawl on the upper part of his body, the leggings of multicolored silk on the lower part of his body, the silken scarf, silken ribbons, and the jacket. He also wears the eight jewel ornaments: the jewel crown, earrings, armlets, bracelets, anklets, belt, and long and short necklaces. He is in union with his consort, the white Vajratopa, who is holding a curved knife and a skull cup. Both of them are dignified by the nine peaceful expressions. With his feet in the vajra posture, he sits as the essence of nondual bliss and emptiness in a sphere of rainbow lights and circles.

In the middle of the moon disc in his heart center is the white letter HUNG around which you should visualize the white-colored, immaculate hundred-syllable mantra chain, radiating rays of light and arranged like a coiled snake. Visualizing the deity is the preparatory power of the support. Next, the power of complete remorse is to feel intense regret, like having swallowed poison, towards all the evil actions and misdeeds that you do or do not remember from the past.

Following that, the main part of the practice is the power of the applied antidote. That is invoking the heart samaya of Vajrasattva, supplicating him with intense longing and devotion by forming this thought: "Guru Vajrasattva, please consider me and all other sentient beings, and purify and cleanse all the misdeeds, downfalls, transgressions, and breaches of samaya that we have created and accumulated in our lifetimes since beginningless samsara."

Thereby, rays of light stream forth from the seed syllable and mantra chain in the heart center of Vajrasattva above your head, filling the sky. The light fulfills the two benefits. Returning, a ceaseless stream of wisdom nectar begins to pour forth. It fills the interior of the body of both the lord and his consort. Gradually two streams of nectar flow down in great measure; the first flows from the vajra of the lord and then also from the lotus of his consort.

Entering through the aperture of Brahma at the top of your head, the stream completely washes the inside and outside of your body. All negative forces in the form of insects, all sicknesses in the form of pus and decomposing blood, and all misdeeds and obscurations in the form of ash and coal-colored liquid, are driven out through your lower openings just as dust is washed away by a mountain stream flooded in spring. Your body takes on the empty and luminous nature of light similar to an immaculate crystal sphere. Imagine that you are again completely filled with nectar; recite the hundred syllables in the manner of a supplication. Exert yourself incessantly as much as you are able. You should complete one hundred thousand along with the additional number. By practicing this visualization of the pouring of the nectar, all your misdeeds, obscurations, faults, downfalls, and breaches of samaya are cleansed and purified.

At the end is the power of resolve and absolution. If you have a strong feeling of remorse for your negative actions, it is a natural law that you will also feel a firm resolve. Resolve therefore from the core of your heart, thinking, "I see the evil of my past actions. From now on, even at the cost of my life, I will not commit any unvirtuous action." Chant *Rudra's Apology,* the *Abhidana of the Samvara Tantra,* with the devotional tune according to your master. Finally, recite the lines of the lamenting apology: "Protector, due to my ignorance and delusion. . ." and so forth, until ". . . child of noble family, all your misdeeds, obscurations, faults, and downfalls are purified."

Thus Vajrasattva relieves and absolves you with his vajra speech, and instructs you by saying, "Henceforth, do not engage in such actions even at the cost of your life." He then melts into light and dissolves inseparably into you. Imagine then that you yourself become the unity of appearance and emptiness in the form of Vajrasattva of Great Bliss. At the end, dissolve the elaborations of the deity and mantra into the innate state of luminosity. Rest in equanimity looking into the natural face of the real Vajrasattva, the aware emptiness in which all the conceptions of something to be purified and something that purifies primordially do not possess any inherent existence. This is the unexcelled way of purifying obscurations by means of the ultimate completion stage. As the conclusion to the practice, dedicate the merit.

When engaging in any kind of recitation, such as the recitation and meditation of Vajrasattva, it is by all means very important not to let your mind wander away from the visualization and not to interrupt the recitation with ordinary talk. In a tantra is said:

If you are lacking in this concentration,
You will have no result even if you recite for aeons,
Just like a boulder submerged in the ocean
[Will never get wet inside].

The benefits are described in the *Immaculate Apology Tantra*:

If you recite one hundred and eight times together the king of all apologies known as the "Hundred Syllables," the quintessence of all the *sugatas* that purifies all breaches and conceptual obscurations, all your breaches will be amended and you will be saved from falling into the three lower realms. The yogi who resolves on it as his daily practice and recites it will be regarded as the noble child of all the buddhas of the three times, and they will keep him under their protection even in that very lifetime. There is no doubt that at the time of death he shall become the foremost son of all the sugatas.

The mandala offering to perfect the accumulations, the positive conditions

> In order to perfect the positive conditions, the accumulations
>   of merit and wisdom,
> Offer the mandalas of the oceanlike realms of the three kayas.

As was said, mandala offerings are praised as being the supreme and wondrous method to completely perfect the two accumulations of merit and wisdom, the positive conditions. In a sutra it says:

> As long as you have not perfected the two supreme
>   accumulations,
> You will not realize the supreme emptiness.

Moreover, it is stated in a tantra:

> If you offer the entire three-thousandfold universe
> Adorned with the desirable qualities
> To all the realms of the enlightened ones,
> You shall perfect the wisdom of the buddhas.

Also Tilopa said:

> Son, until you have realized that the essence
> Of these appearances that arise in dependent connection is
>   beyond origination,
> Never separate yourself, Naropa,
> From the wheels of the chariot of the two accumulations.

The *Dharma Practices of Padma Garwang* describes the time of offering the mandala.

> As to the mandala offerings for the purpose of gathering
>   accumulations,
> Upon the mandala plate of a precious substance, wood or
>   clay,
> Sprinkle the scented water such as cow nectar,
> And arrange the heaps made of precious stones,
>   medicines, and grains.
> Of the two mandalas, the mandala of the shrine and the
>   mandala of the offerings,
> Visualize first the mandala of the shrine.

Having visualized the shrine mandala, the material of the practice mandala plate should be at best of gold or silver; second best is copper or bell metal, or as a last resort an object with a smooth surface such as a flat stone or wooden plate will also be sufficient. The heaps to be placed thereon should at best be precious stones such as turquoise, coral, sapphire, and pearl. Next best are medicinal fruits such as the yellow, beleric, and emblic myrobalan.[11]

Third best are grains such as barley, rice, wheat, or legumes. As a last resort, one can use stones, pebbles, or sand as the support for one's visualization. In any case, polish the surface of the mandala plate thoroughly and begin by placing five heaps upon the practice mandala. The visualization of the filed of accumulations is similar to the visualization for taking refuge, the only difference being that you need not imagine the wish-fulfilling tree.

Gather together the offering mandala and the articles such as precious stones, and so forth, as mentioned above. First polish the plate carefully to symbolize the natural purity of sentient beings. Following that, sprinkle it with drops of cow nectar and perfumed water. This is said to be for the purpose of not letting the moisture of wisdom disappear. Then take a small heap with the thumb and ring finger of your right hand, and, holding the mandala plate with your left hand, imagine that you and all other sentient beings are seated together and with your bodies are placing the heaps of the threefold mandala.

With your voice leading, you are proclaiming the lines of the mandala offering. There are numerous mandala offerings since the Old and New Schools each have their own traditions. In particular, each of the treasures of the Old School itself also has a mandala offering. Here in our own tradition, we practice the mandala offering in the style of the Trikaya Jewel. We should, however, follow the offering that has been widely known here in Tibet, which was composed by the protector of beings, Chögyal Pakpa of the Sakya School. Chant OM VAJRA BHUMI, and so forth, the mantra and the text. When saying OM VAJRA REKHE, arrange the Iron Mountains. Saying, "The king of the mountains, Sumeru," place a big heap in the center, and when saying East Videha, and so forth, place first a heap to the east, which is the direction facing the field of accumulation. Following that, place the jewel mountain to the east as it is the quality of the eastern continent, and in the same way, the wish-fulfilling tree to the south, the wish-granting cow to the west, and the effortless harvest to the north. Of the seven royal possessions, the wheel is to the east, the jewel to the south, the queen to the west, the minister to the north, the elephant to the southeast, the supreme steed to the southwest, and the general to the northwest, in addition to the treasure vase to the northwest. Then, of the eight goddesses, the goddess of grace is to the east; the garland goddess is to the south, the song goddess to the west, the dance goddess to the north, the flower goddess to the southeast, the incense goddess to the southwest, the lamp goddess to the northwest, and the perfume goddess to the northeast. The sun is to the east, and the moon to the west. Finally, place the precious canopy to the south and the banner of complete victory, victorious over all opponents, to the north.

Following that, while saying, "The abundant splendor and riches of gods and humans, without anything lacking," pour, covering everywhere, and then place the top ornament if you have one. Then say, "I offer this to all the sacred root and lineage masters, the yidam assembly of mandala deities, the buddhas and bodhisattvas, the dakinis and Dharma protectors, along with all the assemblies of wealth gods and treasure lords. Out of compassion, please accept it for the benefit of beings. Having accepted it, please bestow your blessings." This was the mandala offering with the elaborate heaps.

According to our own treasure text, next make the offering

by saying, "OM AH HUNG, I and all the infinite beings . . ." and so forth. Finally, say, "OM AH HUNG, The three realms, worlds and beings, splendor and riches . . ." and so forth. Say these lines, and make the offering, imagining the bodies, enjoyments, and the ocean of virtues of yourself and all the infinite sentient beings, in the abundant forms of the Mount Sumeru, the four continents, and the riches of gods and humans. This is the outer relative mandala offering of substantial things. The inner mandala offering of the vajra body is to transform your body—the aggregates, elements, sense bases, sense organs, and the interior—and offer them as offering articles. All these mandala offerings are nothing but your own mental projections. In fact, they do not possess any self-nature in their own respect. Recognizing this is the secret mandala of awakened mind.

With the visualization of offering these three mandalas together, count to the number of one hundred thousand, as well as the additions, of the longer or the condensed of the verses mentioned above. At the end of the session, dissolve the field of accumulation into yourself, and maintain the recognition of your mind's nature.

Through offering these outer, inner, and secret mandalas, you will perfect the accumulation of merit, the means with conceptions, and the special accumulation of wisdom, the knowledge without conceptions. Through this, the conditions necessary for the supreme virtues of the paths and levels to arise in your being will soon present themselves.

When making mandala offerings, it is essential to offer with pure motivation, to keep the offering articles clean, and to make them pleasing. Exerting yourself in a method, such as these mandala offerings, for gathering the accumulations is a vital point of practice that should never be abandoned throughout the duration of the path.

Meditation on the guru yoga of blessings, the root of the path of Vajrayana

> In particular, apply the key points of the essence of all the
> paths,
> The guru yoga of devotion.

This has three parts:

A. Externally, to practice in the manner of supplication.
B. Internally, to practice in the manner of recitation.
C. Secretly, to practice the true guru yoga of simplicity in the manner of action-application.

A. Externally, to practice in the manner of supplication

In this context, the power of experience and realization and the root of all the accomplishments on the path of Vajrayana depend exclusively on the blessings of the sacred guru. The practice of guru yoga is therefore taught in all the tantric scriptures. It is stated that it is superior to all the practices of development and completion. In a tantra it is said:

> Compared to meditating on one hundred thousand deities
> for one million aeons,
> It is superior to remember the guru for just one instant.

In the *Hevajra Tantra,* it says:

> The coemergent that is neither expressed by others
> Nor to be found anywhere else
> Will be known by the timely and skillful teaching of the guru
> And through one's own merit.

Nagarjuna has said:

> When someone is falling from the summit of the king of
> mountains,
> He will still fall though he thinks, "I will not fall."
> When someone has obtained beneficial teachings through
> the kindness of the guru,
> He will still be liberated even though he thinks, "I will not
> be freed."

In the songs of the Great Chetsün, it is stated:

> When someone feels devotion towards the master,
> Certainly, experience and blessings will arise.

The *Array of Ati* mentions:

> The one who meditates on the kind master
> Above his head, in the center of his heart,
> Or in the palm of his hand—
> That person will be the holder
> Of the accomplishments of a thousand buddhas.

Drigung Kyobpa has said:

> If the sun of devotion does not shine
> On the snow mountain of the guru's four kayas,
> The rivers of blessings will not flow.
> Be therefore diligent in devotion.

The Great Master has said:

> There is no happiness in the realm of samsara.
> Endeavor earnestly in accomplishing liberation.
> The excellent guru is the permanent object of refuge.
> Supplicate him continuously from your heart.

Since these statements are all true, the master, who possesses the nature of the Sangha as his body, the Dharma as his speech, and the Buddha as his mind, is the embodiment of all the buddhas of the ten directions and the three times.

Moreover, at this time we lack the fortune of meeting the buddhas of the past and of tasting the nectar of their words. There is nothing present of what they did or taught. Even the Buddha himself did not appear without the support of a master. As is said in the *Profound Path:*

> Although the rays of sunlight are very hot,
> Fire does not occur without a lens.
> Likewise, the blessings of the buddhas also
> Cannot appear without a master.

Consequently, focus your mind with devotion and form this thought: "My own master is superior to and possesses even greater kindness than the buddhas of the ten directions and the three times." Then allow your body and mind to rest in naturalness. Let all your ordinary perceptions of the place where you are dissolve into the space of luminosity. After this, keep the one-pointed devotion that the world is sacred, vividly present as the Lotus Arrayed Realm of Akanishtha. Your dwelling place is sacred, brilliantly displayed as the palace of great liberation, and the inhabitants are sacred, vividly present as the forms of the divine assemblies of vidyadhara masters. While visualizing yourself as the innate deity, whichever is suitable, or as Shri Vajrasattva, recite:

In the sky before me, amidst an ocean of offering clouds . . .

In the sky before you, amidst an ocean of gathered offering clouds, is a precious throne supported by eight great lions. On it is a lotus flower with one hundred thousand petals. On the flower are two discs, the sun and the moon, which are the same size as the pistils.

Seated on the piled seat of these four is the one who in essence is your root guru and in form is the Vajra-Holder of Uddiyana, Mahaguru Padma Tötreng Tsal, the great sovereign who outshines appearance and existence. His body is white in color, with a hue of red. With one face and two arms, he has the expression of peacefully smiling wrath.

With his right hand raised, he points a five-pronged golden vajra into the sky. With his left hand in equanimity, he holds a skull cup of nectar with a vase whose lid ornament is a wish-fulfilling jewel.

On his body, he wears, in layers, the secret white dress, the blue gown, the three yellow and red Dharma robes, and the majestic brown brocade cloak. In the crook of his left arm, he holds his consort Mandarava concealed in the form of a three-pointed khatvanga.

On his head, he wears the *padma tongdröl,* the lotus crown that liberates through seeing. It has a half-vajra top and is ornamented with a vulture feather, silk ribbons, a mirror, and a peacock feather.

With his two feet in the playful royal posture, he is poised majestically within the sphere of appearance and existence as a gathering of rainbow rays, circles, and masses of light.

Above his head, upon a lotus and moon seat, is the vidyadhara Shri Singha whose body color is reddish brown. His right hand points in a threatening gesture at the sky. With his left hand in equanimity, he holds a skull cup filled with nectar. He wears the attire of a yogic practitioner. On his right is the acharya Manjushrimitra and on his left is the great pandita Jnanasutra.

Above the head of Shri Singha is the vidyadhara Prahevajra, Garab Dorje. To his right is Amitabha, and to his left is the Great Compassionate One. Above the head of Prahevajra are Vajrasattva, Vajradhara, and dharmakaya Samantabhadra with consort. They are arranged in tiers, one above the other. They are surrounded by the masters of the Luminous Heart Essence, by the twenty-one adepts, by all the other lineage gurus of the Mind and Space Sections, and by the masters of the outer, inner, and secret cycles of the Instruction Section.

To the right side of Padmakara, upon a lion throne, is the Dharma king known as Vajra Prophesy. He is surrounded by the vidyadhara masters of Lung Anu Yoga such as the three family lords, sons of the conquerors, and the herukas of the five families with their consorts. To the left side, upon a lion throne, lotus, and moon, are Buddhaguhya and the acharya Lilavajra. They are surrounded by the vidyadhara siddhas of development Mahayoga such as the eight vidyadhara masters, and all the great charioteers of the tantra and sadhana Section.

In between all these, seated like assembled cloud banks, are the ones who attained accomplishment in the Kriya, Charya, and Yoga tantras, and the great charioteers of the Tripitaka such as the six ornaments and the two supreme ones.

To the right side of the form of Nangsi Zilnön is the acharya Vimalamitra and to his left side is Bodhisattva Shantarakshita. Around them are seated the Dharma king Trisong Deutsen, Namkhai Nyingpo, Sangye Yeshe, Gyalwa Chog-yang, Drimey Dashar, Langdro Lotsawa, Dorje Dudjom, Vairochana, Prince Yeshe Rölpa Tsal, Yeshe Tsogyal, and the king's subject-disciples, the translators, and panditas. They are again surrounded by a gathering of siddhas who throughout the three times have appeared, are present, or are to appear. This is called the detailed, elaborated version.

In the medium version, you visualize merely the eight Indian vidyadharas, Prahevajra, Shri Singha, King Jah, the five excellent beings, and the eight Tibetan vidyadharas. In the condensed version, there is the tradition for teaching that the main figure alone is sufficient. Even in the condensed version, however, the chief figure has, above his head and surrounding him, an inconceivable ocean of vidyadharas and siddhas from India and Tibet. Together with the three great tertöns, he is seated as being actually present.

To visualize all this is the outer form of practice, "visualizing in the manner of a great gathering." To visualize the three kayas of the dharmakaya Amitabha, the sambhogakaya Great Compassionate One, and the nirmanakaya Padmakara, one above the other, together with the three great tertöns, as being actually present in person, is the inner form of practice, "visualizing in the manner of tiers."

The root guru, Mahaguru Padmakara, embodies all the buddha families. His body is the embodiment of the whole Sangha. His speech is the embodiment of the entire sacred Dharma. Since the expanse of his mind's realization is of one taste with the dharmakaya of all enlightened ones, he is the embodiment of all the yidams and buddhas. His qualities are the embodiment of all the Precious Ones. His activity is the embodiment of all dakinis and Dharma protectors. To visualize him as such is the secret form of practice, "visualizing in the manner of the all-embodying jewel."

In short, he is seated as the great all-encompassing lord who externally is inseparable from the Three Jewels. Internally, he is inseparable from the three roots, and secretly, he is inseparable from the three kayas. He is, consequently, with respect to his qualities, equal to all the buddhas. In his kindness, however, he is superior to all the enlightened ones. Make a firm decision about this, arouse certainty, and think:

"No matter what happens to myself or any of the infinite sentient beings, whether it may be joyful or sorrowful, good or bad, high or low, in whatever you do, Precious Master of Uddiyana, please think of me! Besides you, the root guru, I have no other refuge or hope, protector or helper. Please bless my being by clearing away the obstacles on the path to enlightenment. Increase the virtue of the paths and levels, and ultimately bless me to become inseparable from the three secrets of the supreme vidyadhara guru!"

Maintain this thought and make supplications with intense trust and devotion, placing your complete reliance on him.

Moreover, according to the vajra speech of Padmakara:

"Although there will arise infinite different kinds of obstacles for the ones who try to practice the sacred Dharma correctly, the only method for dispelling them is supplication to the guru. An advice superior to this has not been taught, is not being taught, and will not be taught, even by all the buddhas of the three times. When the obstacles are dispelled, that itself will accomplish the siddhis. Based on that, the paths will also be traversed. It is therefore of great importance, first of all, to supplicate the guru in order to remove the outer, inner, and secret obstacles."

Also he said:

Especially, supplicate in this way in order to remove all
    obstacles.

As was said, recite the *Barchey Lamsel* (Clearing the Obstacles of the Path): [small caps mantra"OM AH HUNG VAJRA GURU PADMA SIDDHI HUNG.] Dharmakaya Amitabha, I supplicate you. . . ." Recite it one hundred, one thousand, ten thousand, or one hundred thousand times—as many as you are able.

The summary of all supplications, the *Six Vajra Lines,* [the Düsum Sangye] beginning with "Buddha of the three times, Guru Rinpoche," you should recite one hundred thousand, times together with the additional number. At the end of each session,

having done as many as you can, such as one hundred, and so
forth, chant also the lineage supplication.

Internally, to practice in the manner of recitation along with receiving the empowerments

Having supplicated in this way, rainbow lights and circles in the
form of bodies, syllables, and attributes appear from the three cen-
ters of each of the figures in the divine assembly. They are countless like specks of dust in a sunbeam and they dissolve into you.
Imagine that you thereby obtain all the empowerments, blessings,
and accomplishments. Endeavor then in reciting the Vajra Guru
mantra as your sole supplication invocation. Do exactly four hundred thousand for each syllable. At times, chant the long or short
supplication, whichever is more suitable.

To conclude the practice of making supplications and reci-
tations, no matter the amount, supplicate while thinking of the
qualities of the root and lineage gurus. Hereby the assembly
comprising the three roots dissolves into the lineage gurus, the
embodiments of all objects of refuge. They then dissolve into the
Precious Master of Uddiyana.

The Guru himself is seated as the embodied essence of the
vajra body, vajra speech, vajra mind, and vajra wisdom of all the
buddhas. At the top of his head, from the letter mantra OM shining like a crystal, white rays of light stream forth and dissolve
into the top of your head. This purifies your bodily karmas, such
as killing and other physical obscurations. You are empowered
to practice the path of the development stage. Imagine that the

good fortune to attain the fruition, the level of nirmanakaya, is established in your being.

Then, red rays of light stream forth from the letter mantra AH, glowing like a lotus ruby in the guru's throat center, and they dissolve into your throat. This purifies verbal karma, such as lying, divisive talk, and other obscurations of speech. You obtain the secret empowerment, and you are empowered to practice the path of *tsa-lung,* the channels and winds. Imagine that you have become endowed with the good fortune to accomplish the fruition, sambhogakaya.

Then, blue rays of light stream forth from the azure-colored mantra HUNG in the heart center of the guru and dissolve into your heart center. This purifies mental karmas, such as wrong views and other obscurations of mind. You obtain the wisdom-knowledge empowerment, and you are empowered to practice the *phonya* path. Imagine that the good fortune to accomplish the fruition, dharmakaya, is established in your being.

Then, multicolored rays of light stream forth from the letter mantra HRIH in the guru's navel center and dissolve into your navel center. This purifies the combined obscurations of your three doors. You obtain the fourth empowerment, and you are empowered to practice the path of Dzogchen. Imagine that the good fortune to accomplish the fruition, the state of *svabhavika-kaya,* is established in your being. Meditate in this way, and receive the empowerments.

The practice of the true guru yoga of simplicity, in the manner of the action-application

Chant, "The Great Master of Uddiyana . . ." and so forth. Due to your intense devotion to the guru, he regards you with an even greater compassion. Thus, with a smiling face and with his eyes gazing passionately, he dissolves joyfully into you. Look into your own mind inseparable from the mind of the guru, the innate and natural face of awareness and emptiness that is free from the complexities of the three times. In other words, your mind free from complexity is dharmakaya. Luminous wakefulness free from fixation is sambhogakaya. The unobstructed basis for manifesting as manifold expressions is nirmanakaya. The inseparability of essence, nature, and compassion is stated by the acharya Lilavajra:

Within basic awareness as essence, nature, and
     compassion,
Is the mandala of all the conquerors, it is taught.
The three kayas are a natural possession.

The *The Tantra of Studded Jewels* mentions:

The perfect buddha is your awareness itself.
Its essence remains unchanged throughout the three times.
Its nature is always without obstruction.
Its compassion is constantly self-manifest.

In the *Talgyur* it is said:

The naturally abiding wisdom
Is inseparable in the manner of three.

It is stated in the *Pearl Garland Tantra:*

> Within the primordial purity of the very beginning,
> There is not even the word *delusion.*
> How can there then be the word *nondelusion?*
> Confusion is therefore primordially pure.

As was stated in these ways, having resolved the ground through the view, you should rest evenly for as long as you can in the state free from all kinds of complex extremes.

Here you can engage in the main practice, in other words, the extensive, medium, or condensed practice manuals for development and completion. Or, if you at this point enter into the activities of your daily life, you should chant the verses for dedication, aspiration, and auspiciousness, beginning with,

> HO
> The virtue of practicing the Secret Mantra of the great
> vehicle.

Concluding practices

One must completely dedicate all the roots of virtue towards supreme enlightenment and seal the practice with pure aspirations. It is said in the *Sutra Requested by Wisdom Ocean:*

> Just as a drop of water falling into the great ocean
> Is not exhausted before the ocean is exhausted,

Likewise, the virtue that has been fully dedicated towards
    enlightenment
Will not be exhausted as long as enlightenment is not
    attained.

In that way, you should exert yourself at all times in dedicating your virtue to the benefit of all sentient beings. Dedicate all
the virtues gathered throughout the three times by yourself and
others, exemplified by your present virtuous practice, while giving it the seal of nonconceptual knowledge as in the case of the
complete dedication of Manjushri Kumara.

You should also train yourself in the general three yogas of con-
tinual practice. Thus, you must train in spending your time acting
in accordance with the Dharma in all the activities of your daily
life. Especially, offer to the master the first part of your food and
drink, regarding it as having the nature of nectar, and offer him
your clothing, thinking them to be divine garments. No matter
what occurs within your six sense perceptions, be it good or bad,
pleasant or unpleasant, do not give way to ordinary thoughts, but
maintain continuously awareness manifestations of deity, mantra,
and wisdom.

When about to lie down in the evening, chant supplications
for the sake of yourself and others, such as *Sampa Lhündrub*,
(Spontaneous Fulfillment of Wishes) and *Barchey Lamsel*. In particular, chant the *Aspiration for Purifying the Realm of the Three
Kayas*. Afterwards, the guru at the top of your head comes down
through the aperture of Brahma and appears within your heart

center, which is in the form of a four-petaled lotus flower. The light rays from him illuminate totally the interior of your body. Direct your mind to that and go to sleep, maintaining the continuity of practice, the state in which the guru's mind and your own are inseparably mingled. Alternatively, the rays of light hit the outer world that is visualized as a celestial palace. The world then melts into light like salt left in water and dissolves into the inner inhabitants of sentient beings who are visualized as deities. They then dissolve into you, and you into the guru in your heart center. He then dissolves into nonconceptual luminosity.

Rest then, without being interrupted by other thoughts, in the state of inner luminosity, the dissolved yet unobscured nakedness of aware emptiness. If you happen to wake from that, cut the flow of thinking such as subtle discursiveness and dreaming. Maintain the all-pervading and natural brilliance of luminosity. Through this, you will attain the luminosity of the sleeping state and recognize dreaming. After that, practice, as previously explained, the "yoga of getting up at dawn," and then engage in the other of the four sessions.

In general, even at the time of practicing the main part, the preliminaries are never to be cast away. Especially, when practicing development and completion, it is essential to practice without interruption the receiving of the four empowerments by means of the guru yoga at the beginning of each session. In short, by perfecting this path of the preliminaries with pure devotion and samaya, you will, without depending upon the main part of practice, be assured to go the Glorious Mountain of Chamara. In that pure realm it is certain that you will reach the supreme vidy-

adhara level swifter than the course of the sun and moon, through
the path of the four vidyadharas.

> Exemplified by the merit of writing this lucid and concise
>   guidebook
> To the sections of accomplishing supreme enlightenment
>   through the preliminaries
> Of the profound instruction *Dispeller of All Obstacles,*
> Which is exalted among the one hundred million guru
>   practices,
> May all the virtue accumulated throughout the three times
> Cause myself and the entire ocean of sentient beings filling
>   the sky
> To be accepted until enlightenment
> By the Dharma king of Uddiyana, the union of the three
>   kayas.

Although I made some notes on what little remained in the
field of my mind from the time I received thoroughly the ripening and liberating profound instructions from the lips of the
All-Knowing King of Dharma, the venerable and supreme master, they were left unedited. Later on, I received on the crown of
my head the insistent command from the precious reincarnation
of Tsangsar Ngaktrin Lama, Karma Ngawang Samten Yeshe
Gyatso,[12] who is the divine son of the one who appeared as the
daughter of the bloodline of the great master and treasure revealer
himself. When, in addition, I received requests from some faith-
ful disciples not to turn my back on them, I took the notes men-

tioned above as the basis and ornamented them a little with the immaculate preliminaries of the Early Translation School [the Old School]. Other than that, I do not myself possess any accomplishments or qualities that could merit a composition. Yet, without falling prey to distortions, self-seeking, and bloated arrogance, this was written in the residence of the lord, the Vajra-Arrayed Palace of Secret Mantra at Ridge of Sages (Neten Gang). It was written with the thought of benefiting a few beggars like myself, by the insensitive tramp known as Padma Gyurme Kunzang Tekchok Tenpel Ngedön Dewey Dorje Chokley Namgyal, who eagerly partakes in the misdeeds of living off donations. I walk at the end of the line of the Dharma lineage of the great master and treasure revealer and was born in the family line of the lord's brother. May this be a cause for all beings to attain the level of the Ever Excellent Vidyadhara Master.

SARVA MANGALAM. May all be auspicious!

The Mind Ornament of Padma

An Explanation of the "Vajra-Verse Supplication"

Kyabje Dudjom Rinpoche

OM SVASTI

Having paid homage to the lord guru,
The wish-fulfilling jewel who dispels our misery when we
    think of him,
I will let my words open up a small understanding of the
    meaning
Of the Vajra-Verse Supplication.

The supplication is stated in these words:

Precious guru, Buddha of the triple times,
Mahasukha Lord of all accomplishments,
Wrathful Strength, mara-tamer of all hindrances,
We call on you, bestow your blessings here.
Calm the outer, inner, and the secret hindrances.
Bless us, naturally fulfill our every aim.

I will now clarify a little of the meaning of these vajra words
of Guru Rinpoche himself, the quintessence of all supplications
revealed in the profound treasures of Orgyen Chokgyur Lingpa,
by explaining it in accordance with the regular teachings of
Kunkhyen Lama Dorje Ziji Tsal from the oral instructions of my
family lord, Gyurmey Ngedön Wangpo.

Precious guru, Buddha of the triple times

Externally, this means the precious Buddha among the Precious
Ones, because Orgyen Rinpoche himself is the master who is
inseparable from the three mysteries of all the buddhas appearing

throughout the past, present, and the future. Internally, it means the guru, the root of blessings, among the three roots, because Orgyen Rinpoche himself is the general wisdom form of all the gurus of the mind, sign and hearing lineages. Secretly, it means the dharmakaya among the three kayas, because he is primordially present as emptiness endowed with all the supreme aspects possessing the indivisible nature of the kayas and wisdoms.

Mahasukha Lord of all accomplishments

Externally, this means the sacred precious Dharma, because all the virtues of the truly high and the definite goodness originate from practicing in accordance with the words of the guru. Internally, it means the yidam, the root of siddhis, because all the common and supreme siddhis without exception originate from Guru Rinpoche himself. Secretly, it means the sambhogakaya, because he enjoys all the phenomena of samsara and nirvana as unconditioned great bliss in the manner of nonduality, without moving away from dharmakaya.

... tamer of all hindrances

Externally, this means the precious Sangha, because the dispelling of all the obstacles for the five paths and ten bhumis, as well as the origination of all virtues, depends upon the Sangha, the companions on the path who, again, originate by means of Orgyen Rinpoche. Internally, it means the dakini and *dharmapala,* the roots of activity, because they clear away the practitioner's obstacles on the paths and bhumis and accomplish favorable conditions by means of the four activities. They, too, originate through Orgyen Rinpoche himself, because he is the main figure in all mandalas. Secretly, it means the nirmanakaya, because he emanates in bodily forms, taming by any means necessary, within the perceptions of the various higher, inferior, or mediocre disciples. He establishes them on the paths of ripening and liberation after having taught all the essential points of the profound and extensive teachings to suit their intellects.

In this way, the one who externally is the nature of the Three Precious Ones, internally the nature of the three roots, and secretly the nature of the three kayas, the chief form of all the buddhas, the source of all the sacred teachings, the crest ornament of the entire Sangha and who is the great lord encompassing all families, he is the one who holds the secret name, the

Wrathful Strength, mara-tamer . . .

Why is that? It is because he spontaneously tamed the terrifying four *maras,* delivered the three secret enemies into *dharmadhatu,* and liberated himself through realization. Since he has attained mastery over the four activities, he liberates others out of loving kindness by means of the unceasing compassion of eliminating and cherishing. Thus, through his power of great wisdom endowed with the twofold purity, he liberates the two obscurations, along with habitual patterns, into the state of nondual space and awareness.

To the guru who possesses such qualities,

We call on you . . .

Externally, approach the desired aim of quickly achieving the supreme and common siddhis by supplicating him with the intense power of devotion and longing. Internally, accomplish Guru Rinpoche's level by acknowledging the fact that your three doors primordially are the mandalas of his body, speech, and mind. Secretly, supplicate by applying the activities and maintaining the unfabricated continuity of self-awareness in its natural state—the real means of resolving the fact that the guru is nothing other than your mind-essence endowed with the nature of the four kayas and five wisdoms.

By having supplicated in this way,

. . . bestow your blessings here.

This means, "Please bless me to accomplish the vajra body, the apparent yet empty body, after having been blessed with the guru's body in my body. Please bless me to accomplish the vajra speech, the resounding yet empty speech, after having been blessed with the guru's speech in my speech. Please bless me to accomplish the vajra mind, the aware yet empty mind, after having been blessed with the guru's mind in my mind."

We call on you, bestow your blessings here.

All the conditions averse to accomplishing enlightenment are called obstacles. Outer obstacles are the sixteen major fears: the earth fear of pride, the water fear of desire, the anger fear of fire, the envy fear of wind, the lightning fear of thunderbolts, the weapon fear of what is sharp and piercing, the tyrant fear of prisons, the enemy fear of bandits and thieves, the ghost fear of flesh-eaters, the wrath fear of elephants, the beast fear of lions, the poison fear of snakes and so on, the illness fear of plague and so on, the fear of untimely death, the fear of poverty and scarcity, and the fear of vanishing sense pleasures. Thus, these are the sixteen. Inner obstacles are the four maras, the aggregate mara of ego-clinging, the *klesha* mara of desire and attachment, the godly son mara of deception, and the Lord of Death mara of snatching one's life away. Secret obstacles are the kleshas of the five poisons: desire, anger, stupidity, pride, and envy.

What do they cause obstacles to? They cause obstacles to accomplishing liberation and the state of omniscience. For this reason, supplicate, asking that all outer obstacles may be pacified by the power of the realization that sights, sounds, and awareness are the display of deities, mantras, and dharmakaya; that all inner obstacles may be pacified by liberating grasping and fixation into the space of egolessness; and that secret obstacles may be pacified by the power of realizing that the five poisons are the five wisdoms and taking adverse conditions as the path.

Bless us, naturally fulfill our every aim.

Concerning wishes, there are temporary wishes and ultimate wishes. As to the first, supplicate, for as long as enlightenment has not been attained, to accumulate the conditions conducive to accomplishing it. These are stated as follows:

Long life span, and likewise no sickness,
A handsome form, good fortune, and class,
Wealth and intelligence; thus seven.

Supplicate that you may be sustained by these seven qualities
of a high rebirth, and especially that your being may be enriched
by the seven noble riches. The seven noble riches are the richness
of faith, the richness of discipline, the richness of diligence, the
richness of modesty, the richness of learning, the richness of generosity, and the richness of intelligence.

The ultimate wish is called the supreme siddhi of Mahamudra.
Concerning this, the ground that is the mind-essence of all sentient
beings, the *sugatagarbha,* abides primordially as the nature of buddhahood. Yet, without recognizing sugatagarbha, your natural face,
you become veiled by the two obscurations and habitual patterns
and then wander through samsara. Therefore, practice the path,
the unity of the two accumulations or the unity of the development
and completion stages, as the remedy for these two obscurations.
Consequently, the fruition is to realize the natural state as it is after
purifying the passing stains of this naturally pure mind-essence
endowed with the nature of the four kayas and five wisdoms into
dharmadhatu. This is called the attainment of the supreme siddhi.
Therefore, supplicate, "Quickly and without depending upon effort
and struggle, please bless me with the automatic and spontaneous
fulfillment of all my temporary and ultimate wishes!"

The supreme swift path, the most eminent of all,
Is this excellent guru supplication.

Adhere to it, you who long
For all the goodness and desirable things of this life and of
    the future.
Through the virtue of exerting myself in this way, may I
    and other beings
Be accepted by Guru Rinpoche in all our lives
And with the fulfillment of the wish for the two benefits,
May the goodness of welfare and happiness flourish.

Due to the inquiry and request from the qualified knowledge-lady Tseten Turquoise Lamp, the vidyadhara aspirant, Jigdral Yeshe Dorje, freely wrote this in the Wish-Fulfilling Lion Cave at Paro Taktsang in Bhutan. SIDDHI RASTU.

Notes

1. More details are found in *The Life and Teachings of Chokgyur Lingpa* (Rangjung Yeshe Publications, 1988).
2. Later, in the visualization of the lineage masters, he is called Murub Tsenpo.
3. A mountain in Eastern Tibet that has the shape of a wrathful deity. It is situated on the highway between Jyekundo and Shonda in Quinghai Province.
4. *The Magical Net of the Vidyadhara Gurus (Bla ma rig 'dzin sgyu 'phrul drva ba zhi khro rnam par rol pa'i rgyud kyi rgyal po chen po)* is one of the eight major divisions of Mahayoga tantras. The tantra that is the basis for the *Barchey Künsel* cycle of teachings is *Sheldam Nyingjung*.
5. *Sgyu 'phrul sde brgyad.* Eight major aspects of the tantras of Mahayoga.
6. *Sgrub sde bka' brgyad.* Eight aspects of the sadhanas of Mahayoga.
7. The method for liberation through reading, together with several explanations, will appear in *The Lotus Essence Tantra* (Rangjung Yeshe Translations).
8. The translation, by Erik Pema Kunsang, of this important sadhana, *The Tukdrub Trinley Nyingpo*, together with several commentaries, is available from Rangjung Yeshe Translations..
9. This practice is entitled "The Concise Manual for Daily Practice."
10. The short version consists of the sections of refuge and bodhicitta from "The Concise Manual for Daily Practice." The liturgy for Vajrasattva is the same as in the original, but omits the long "Lamenting Confession of Rudra." The mandala offering is a five-line liturgy. The guru yoga visualization is followed by the supplication entitled "Düsum Sangye"

and the Vajra Guru mantra, and it concludes with four lines each for receiving the empowerments and resting in naturalness. The dedication, aspiration, and lines of auspiciousness are the same as in "The Concise Manual for Daily Practice."

11. Rare fruits from India.

12. This is a reference to Samten Gyatso, the root guru of Tulku Urgyen Rinpoche. For his story, see *Blazing Splendor* (Rangjung Yeshe Publications, 2005).